THE RAMBLINGS OF A
DODGY BLIND POET

for those who love a difference

THE RAMBLINGS OF A DODGY BLIND POET

Written and illustrated by
Adrian Darron

The Ramblings of a Dodgy Blind Poet
Adrian Darron

Published by Greyhound Self-Publishing 2020
Malvern, Worcestershire, United Kingdom.

Printed and bound by Aspect Design
89 Newtown Road, Malvern, Worcs. WR14 1PD
United Kingdom
Tel: 01684 561567
E-mail: allan@aspect-design.net
Website: www.aspect-design.net

Cover Design Copyright © 2020 Aspect Design
Original illustration Adrian Darron Copyright © 2020
ISBN 978-1-909219-69-4

Dedicated to my late mum
'Giving all with no tears, giving all with no fuss'
and lifelong friends
Alev, Linds and Em
with a special thanks to Alice T

A tale can't tell
What a poet can yell
A newspaper writes a view
Where a poem can really show
They make a point
It becomes clear in your head
When you read as a verse
What the TV has never said

AD

CONTENTS

FOR THOSE ABOUT TO START

THERE'S A GIRL

There's a girl in the coffee shop. Do you see her?
That's right, just over there
With her head hung low, her hands in her lap
Sunk down in the soft leather chair

She seems so quiet, she's not looking up
Could she be contemplating
Maybe she's meditating
I'm convinced she's in prayer

I know I shouldn't
But I couldn't help but stare
At the dejection and the loneliness
Of the girl in the soft leather chair

Maybe she's praying for some sad news she's got
Maybe she's praying for the grief to stop
Maybe she's praying every day for her lot
Maybe I shouldn't care, I don't know her
I shouldn't give a jot

But I worry about the girl in the comfy leather seat
Maybe she has no one to confide in
No one to talk to
No one coming in for her to meet

Should I get up? See how she is? Hear her woes?
My heart says I should
My brain wasn't sure
But what have I to lose?

But as I rise I see an emotion flicker across her lips
A brief snigger, a gasp, a groan, a sigh can be heard to emit
When I suddenly realised my mistake
As she looks over here with a smile about to break

Her hands weren't in her lap
Closed together in prayer
She was holding on to something
Much more familiar

She wasn't in the coffee shop
With no one to talk to on her own
She was in the coffee shop
Pressing buttons on her mobile phone

She wasn't feeling bad and oh so sad
Waiting for someone to off load
She was communicating with her online friends
The millions around the globe

She's got Instagram, Facebook, twitter, Watsap, Snapchat
She's got them all, she's got the lot
Whereas what have I got
As I try to smile back; I feel such a clot
It's not the girl over there in the soft leather chair
Sitting on her own
It's the fool over here on the sofa
Drinking coffee, lounging forlorn and all alone
Mmm...

FROM CURRY TO CUSTARD

My friend makes a lovely curry
It's the best I've ever tasted
But when she tries to make custard
Well; most of it gets wasted

Her fingers choose with consummate ease
The condiments her dish sympathetically needs
From Korma to Vindaloo
From Tikka Masala to Saag Aloo

She conjures up a spicy profusion
A combination she stirs to a magical contusion
The taste is exquisite
The tingle is explicit

The prickle to my senses
The sharp tang to my brain
The richness of the creation lay before me
The goodness she produces is hard to explain

The flavours of India and the Orient
Burst on my tongue
A warming taste that's only right not wrong
A welcoming feast that can't be outdone

But when it comes to custard
And my favourite dessert sauce
She adds the same ingredients
She says Its silly not to
Well she would of course

However I don't want chilli mixed with castor sugar
Or vanilla spliced with garam masala
This spicy blend; it doesn't work
To eat anymore I think I'll go berserk

If I try to tell her it goes over her head
If I try to stop her she just goes ahead
She can't leave well alone
The well-stocked spice rack that hangs in her home

You'd think she'd understand
When I say face to face
That the custard she serves
lacks a certain palatable grace

I know I sound a bore
I wonder if I should say more
Perhaps I should say less
I don't want to put her under unnecessary duress

But the next time we have a meal
I'll try to make her a sensible deal
I won't put the custard in the bin
If she agrees to serve it
Ready made from a plastic pot or tin

CONFUSION

I worry about myself sometimes
The things that I do
Ordinary jobs I perform everyday
I get so confused

My body tells me it's right
But my mind hasn't a clue.
I try to remember what I've just been asked
But I need a repeat

Even for the smallest of tasks
My memory sometimes takes a beating
I sometimes forget to turn off the heating
And I've become so poor

At remembering to lock the bathroom door
I'm now so clumsy
I'm afraid to move
If I turn one way I knock over a pot

The other way a glass I dislodge
I apologise to a tree
I say sorry to a post
I swear my gate has said sorry to me

I spill everything I try to carry
I drop stuff on the floor
I'm afraid I'll do it forever more
I say the wrong words at the wrong time
It shouldn't have come out that way
That's not what I meant
That wasn't the line

I really need to engage my brain
Maybe I should just go back to bed
Go to sleep
Wake up at ten and start the day again

REGRET?

I'm standing in a room
In a flat I purchased at the beginning of June
When I first saw it I thought it was neat
But now that I'm here
I now smell the wreak
It has damp in the walls
It has damp under the floor
The carpet is decaying
Of the pile there is no more
And it's not a nice feeling
When you see spiders dangling from the ceiling
Where there's an infestation of ants
And a place where cockroaches and beetles
Are learning to dance
You know I really don't like complaining
And it may not be much
But the toilet has decided it's not going to flush
I'm having to throw water from a pail
I'm fairly sure prisoners and convicts
Are much better off in jail
Cold wind is blowing
Through the bottom of the door
I'm not sure I want to be here anymore
Of course the windows are single
No double glazing here
Was it a mistake to have bought it
As condensation drips from the dirty glass
Much like my fear
But at least I have heating
And the waters tepidly hot
I know I should be grateful

Because I know it's all I've got
I've called in the plumber
And a carpenter for the floor
The plasterers are here skimming
A pretty good job so far
It's costing me a fortune
A pretty penny alas
But once the work is done
I'll bring in all my furniture
And move in my loving class
I'm standing in a room
In a flat I purchased at the beginning of June
I'm looking very pleased
I'm hoping to move in so very soon

REBEL YELL!

Oh! If only I'd been a rebel when I was at school

I don't mean the bully
The jock, the nerd the shy one
Or the apple pet the favourite of all
To have done what rebels did
Oh yes it would have been so cool

I'd have dispensed with the trousers
Tie, black shoes and blazers
And donned jeans, leather jacket
T shirts and trainers
I'd have worn my hair in a disapproving style
A crew cut, a top knot a Viking chic, A pompadour
Or the ever popular low and high fade pile

I would have missed lessons I didn't like
Smoked behind the sheds
Where we stored our bikes
Sneaked off cross-country running
Taken a short cut, hopped on a bus
Ding-ding
Oh yes, I'd have been so cunning

If only I'd been a rebel when I was at school

I'd have skived off, played truant
Used false ID at the corner shop
Blagged a few cans, cadged a fag
And sort of borrowed a fiver from my dad

At the park we'd have played around
Had a laugh, been a fool
Acted like a jerk, having a lark
But when it got late
I'd have to get home
Because I'd hate to admit it
But I'm afraid of the dark

I'd be sent to the headmasters office
I'd be given detention
Amongst my peers
I'd have the sole attention
I'd have gained loyalty
I'd have had full respect
All would have seen me led out of the class
By my ear or the scruff of my neck

RIGHTS FOR THE
CHILDREN, NOT FIGHTS
FOR EDUCATION

I'd have sauntered along the main hall
I'd have been the leader of a posse
Boss of a sombre bunch
My place reserved
At the beginning of the queue
Outside the tuck shop
The refectory, waiting for lunch

If only I'd been a rebel when I was at school

I'd have been the anarchist, the malcontent
Outside the school rules for justice I'd torment
I'd have spoken out loudly
Debated and argued with the teachers
The masters, the governors, the leeches

I'd have jousted for the right
For the young and the weak
The scared and the lonely
I'd have been Citizen Smith of the day
Mahatma Ghandi of the moment
Che Guevara of my time
Luke Skywalker of the classroom

Oh! If only

If only I'd been a rebel when I was at school

I'd have organised pickets
Outside the school latrines
Arranged hunger strikes in the canteen
Sit ins in the sports dome
Waving placards and banners
Slogans and demands we'd have creatively honed

I'd have been the pupil
That would have raised some hell
Synonymous with strife and trouble
You could tell
With relief at the end of the day
The teachers would heavily sigh, smile heartily
And been glad at the toll of the final bell

If only I'd have been a rebel when I was at school

Would it have been so bad
Had I been a little tougher
Would I have enjoyed youth more
Had a little more laughter

But looking back in retrospect
I was never the rebel
But I was never the bully, the jock
The nerd, the quiet one
Or the apple pet, the favourite of all
I was just known quite simply as

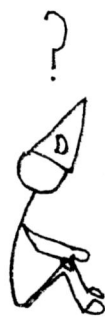

Well......the schoolyard fool

Oh! If only I'd been a rebel when I was at school

We'd have all shouted out

REBELS RULE!

REBELS YELL!

WORK......?

Work, work. Why do we work?
Is it for the money? Is it for the prestige?
Is it for the yearning of something to do?
Is it for something that's expected of you?
Is it for the love of someone that's new?

It seems such a waste
It seems such a chore
Up every morning, it's all the same
It seems quite clear
Oh it's a drear oh what a bore

We wish the seconds, the minutes to go by
We wish the hours, the days to just slide by
We could be doing something different
We could be doing other things
No! Then again, maybe that's a lie

We like to read, we like to write
We'd like to sleep all day
We'd prefer to sleep our time away
We'd like to sing, we'd like to dance
We prefer our hobbies
If only we had the chance

For years we've worked at the same places
Sitting at the same desks
Seeing the same faces
Hearing the same voices
The same insignificant conversations
All of the time

"good morning, how are you?"
"hi, you ok, alright?"
"yep, no worries, no problems"
"fine, doing ok, how are you? Are you ok?"
"yes I'm fine, I'm alright"

The same insignificant conversations
All of the time

Maybe we should leave the road
Get on the pavement, live off the street
Beg for money, pick up the odd penny
Become a layabout, a scrounger, a cheat

Just for once we'll be early
Just for once we should be late
Maybe we'll miss the train,
Catch the following bus

Who really cares,
We won't be missed
No one will give a fu##
No one will kick up a fuss

Maybe we'll inherit
Let the past bequeath us
Let those who've come before
Do the drudge just to please us
A house in the garden of Eden
A mansion in the southern east of Kent
Allow us to live the realm, like a king
No mortgage, no bills, certainly no rent

Work, work, why do we work?
Is it for the money? Is it for the prestige?
Is it for the yearning of something to do?
Is it for something that's expected of you?
Is it for the love of someone that's new?

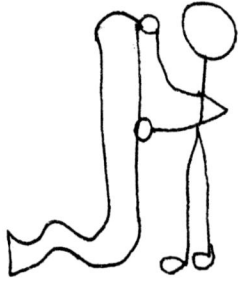

WHY SO LONG?

I know my poems are long
Yes I know, they go on and on and on and on
But stick with them for a little while
In the end they'll make you smile

Leave a large part of your day
For these extremely arduous tasks
Make some sandwiches, bake a cake
Get a coffee in a humongous flask

Lock the door
Turn off the phone
Reject all visitors
Now it's time to be on your own

Word after word, verse after verse
Once you start you just can't finish
You may forget to eat
You may forget to drink
You won't be able to sleep
You may get quite thinnish

I warn you get ready for a marathon read
I'm sure it's something you really need
Why are my poems long?
Well they usually are
They normally go on and on and on and on

However count yourself lucky
This one's quite short
This one's just a note
A quote that's tiny
So now it's time for me
To quickly sign off and then depart

GOING BLIND

It's a really dark place when you first lose your sight
Taking a step fills you with fright
Your lungs and heart feel so tight
Something's not right
You can't stand up straight
Your balance you've got to fight
Your world has ended
You're in plight
But you soon learn to cope
You realise there's hope
Your hearing becomes clearer
Your environment gets nearer
Though you can't see
You can still touch humanity
Your body and brain come about
You realise you can reach out
With a little bit of fortitude
And a little bit of help
Your senses come alive
You have the drive
You can still scream and shout
It's a really dark place when you first lose your sight
But now you see the light
The futures so bright
Will you survive
Well I think you just might

THE LEGEND OF ALICE T

I BELIEVE IN ALICE

(part one)

I believe in Alice when she says the world is flat
I believe in the illusion of magic
Sawing a person in half
Pulling a rabbit out of a hat
I believe in producing a coin from behind an ear
I believe though I watched, it still wasn't clear
I believe in leprechauns and hobgoblins
I believe at the end of a rainbow finding a golden pot
I believe in fairies at the bottom of the garden
Trolls under the bridge
Lying patiently in wait to gobble you up
The creature under the bed
The boogie man in the cupboard
Who I believe even now has never been discovered
I believe in unicorns and dragons
On releasing the kraken
I believe in not walking under a ladder
Or the cracks on a pavement
And not working on Friday the 13th
Staying in bed and hiding under the sheets
I believe in flying saucers and learning how to duck
But I also believe in a four leaf clover
A rabbits foot
Nailing a horseshoe to a wall
I believe in picking up a penny
And all day you'll have better luck
I believe in throwing salt over my left shoulder
I believe we won't get any older
I believe in the Loch Ness Monster
In the Harpy

In the abominable Snowman
The mythical Centaur
I believe dinosaurs still roam the land
In visiting Peter Pan in neverneverland
I believe in the Grinch ruining Christmas
The well behaved and naughty lists
I believe in Santa and his Elves
I believe in Rudolph ringing silver bells
I believe in God in heaven
The devil in hell
I believe in angels protecting us
As we go through struggles
In living in Hogwarts with Harry Potter and a muggle
I believe in witches on broomsticks with pointed hats
Stirring a bubbling brew in a cauldron
Adding drops of blood taken from a bat
I believe in ghosts, spirits and ghouls
I also believe in vampires
Zombies and werewolves
I believe in wishing on a star
Driving through the air in a flying car
I believe every cloud has a silver lining
And everything creepy that happens in the shining
I believe carrots allow you to see in the dark
I believe we should all look forward, never back
I believe crusts make you hair curly
I believe in the Easter bunny and the tooth fairy
I believe sugar helps the medicine go down
In the oh so sad tears of a clown
I believe in men from Mars
In people from outer space
I believe aliens live amongst us
Walking the streets; having a place

I believe the moon is made of blue cheese
And the stars are made of shiny peas
I believe the universe may one day get up and leave
I believe everyone on this planet should live in peace
I believe the earth should always try and never cease
I believe in Alice when she says the world is flat
I certainly do
I believe in all of this
And I also believe in most of that

I BELIEVE IN ALICE

(part two)

I believe in Alice when she says the world is flat
I believe in her honesty and having a great chat
I believe in a loving kiss
I hope and believe I'll always be missed
I believe in saying excuse me after you sneeze
I believe in a thank-you and a please
I believe in not swearing
It doesn't sound caring
I believe in keeping all animals safe
In believing in the human race
I believe in having a smile on your face
And allowing it to reach your eyes
I believe our longed for love will one day walk on by
I believe eating an apple a day keeps the doctor away
And children should get up
Go outside and play
I believe in everything a politician says
I believe in having guilty pleasures
And keeping safe all my other secret treasures
I believe in singing in the rain
Any other time is just not the same
I believe in dancing away the night
In parents when they say they are always right
I believe in love at first sight, finding a soul mate
I believe in the excitement of a first date
And taking a chance on a blind date
I believe in keeping a promise
Never breaking a vow
I believe in the here and now
I believe life has a purpose

In the joy of a circus
I believe in the sound of silence
Blocking out the noise around us
I believe in not thinking twice and everyone is nice
I believe in the five second rule
Being kind and never cruel
I believe in taking a leap of faith
As our friends will always keep us safe
I believe all great things come in small packages
Much easier to handle
Far less baggage
I believe in fate and having to wait
Forming an orderly queue
I believe in starving a cold and feeding the flu
In tossing a dice and taking a chance on a second glance
I believe we should look after our environment
I still believe in being a polite gent
In opening a door and allowing you to go first
In drinking plenty, quenching your thirst
I believe we should be ourselves
And not be bullied by social media trolls
I believe the patience over a jigsaw puzzle
In not having to struggle
I believe in the strength of an anti-biotic
But I believe we could learn not to rely upon it
I believe we should never tease
As we all have knobbly knees
I believe in enjoying a joke
And having a bubble bath
I believe in the power of soap
Enjoying an aromatic soak
I believe in hanging loose
The choices we choose

I believe we should stop all the worlds abuse
I believe in the emotions we feel
In staying real
I believe we should never steal
I believe in the good neighbours we've been sent
I believe in returning what's been lent
I believe in stopping all crime
I believe in all of this in time
I believe when Alice says the world is flat
Don't you?
Don't we all believe in that?

FOR THOSE OF AN
AGE DO YOU DARE
READ AND ENGAGE

(TAKE A DEEP BREATH AND HOLD ON TO YOUR HATS)

49 AND A LITTLE OVER ¾S

The form requests the usual info
Name, address, email and mobile
But the question I wished to delay
Had only three letters I hoped not to betray

Will it make a difference if I leave it out?
Will it make a difference if I rub it out?
Will it really matter? I ask you in frustration
Tell me why should I put it? What is it all about?

I'll say sorry I didn't see it
I never noticed it can't be true
I'll blame my eyesight, I'll just deny it
Those three small letters
It's asking at the end of the 5th row

It's not IOU or TOL or HRT or even LOL
It's AGE I see in front of me
I'll say I simply forgot
I just don't know

I refuse to believe I'm over half a century
I've not reached that time
Despite all the facts and all the other sources
I'm only 49 and a little over ¾s

I'll not agree with what my passport is showing me

The truth is laid out bare
All the evidence is there
My body has betrayed me
It's so unfair

What was once up north
Has suddenly, slowly slipped down south
The bingo and bat wings hang below
The chin is heavy and oh so low

My boobs have gone to my navel
To my knees have gone my bum
And whatever happened to my abs?
My tight firm six pack flat tum

It can't be right, something is wrong
I won't allow it, I won't follow the orders
Cause I'm only 49 and a little over ¾s

I cannot for the life of me see
What my mirror is reflecting to me

My eyesight is poor
My hearing is failing
My hairs a blue rinse
It could do with the grey shading

My teeth are my own, I'm delighted to mention
However they're turning and fading
And needing some well thought out work
And some polite but sorry to say
Orthodontic cosmetic persuasion

My memory is going, it's worse every day
Sometimes I forget
Am I at work?
Or am I a child and supposed to be at play

We're having a coffee, you're talking to me
I must look confused, it just can't be
I'm choking up, I'm feeling blue
It's no good, I have to ask
"excuse me if I sound rude but tell me again
who the flipping heck are you?"

My children say mum look after yourself
Checking bumps and lumps is important to your health
Attend all the tests, take all the scans
As you are important and inclusive
In our families future plans

My blood test reveals diabetes on the borders
But that's no good to me
When I'm only 49 and a little over ¾s

But I hear and I'll take note
Of what my doctor and my children are telling me

One minute I'm sad, the next I'm happy
One minute I feel on top of the world
The next I'm shouting, angry and crappy
The realisation hits me, you can see how I know

I've reached the middle of the road
My hormones are driving me crazy
I have these terrible mood swings
I feel I'm in mid flow

It's a wonder I can still cope
As the world turns so fast
And at other times so damn slow
And as if that wasn't enough
I'm now working through, by day and by night
The predictable but inevitable menopausal hot flush

He assesses the dramas played out on the sofas
But I'm not listening as I'm only 49 and a little over ¾s

I don't think I can take in
How the poor psychologist is confusing me

My partner to help me out, to help him as well
Took me shopping, but would you believe it
WELL!
It was such a surprise
We went straight into a shop
With DIY DVDs and erotic magazines

And other
I've never, goodness seen such naughty things
Strange devices with batteries and electronic secrets
Dildos of rubber
Clothes of spandex and leather

And other sheer garments
That somehow adheres and clings
But I'll certainly never wear them
No, I'll hardly go there
In those invisible, wispy g strings

He's hoping I guess for some favourable chances
But he'll be lucky, I'm not in the mood
Though I'm only 49 and a little over ¾s

I can't agree with what my husband
Is asking and requesting of me

Sometimes I wish I was young to start again
But looking back as I recall
I didn't like youth that much after all

The pressures put upon at such an age
Are difficult and problematic at any stage
From greasy skin to languid hair
To spots on face to the monthly scare
Looking up to the fashionistas
We hoped one day to emulate and wish for
Buying cloths in sizes we believe we were
But in truth are an impossible fit
Though we try to squeeze
They were impossible to wear

Living up to models standards
Five foot ten and a slim waist
Legs up there and the right face
Taking selfies at a fast pace

Becoming a celebrity
Marrying into royalty
To aspire to a footballers loyalty
To live like a wag
No! The burdens too much

They could do with some drugs
They crave the odd fag
And where is that bottle of vodka
They hid from their dad

Everything's expensive they don't earn enough
They need too much, the list goes on
Make-up, cosmetics, shampoo, hair dye
A weekly trip to the salon

Hair coiffured, nails painted
Eyebrows and private places sainted
You know what I mean
Oh! Come on
Swiping right, swiping left
There's too much choice
They've had enough, they're left bereft

The rent is up, quarterly bills are too
To go anywhere, they're scraping for the fare
Securing a mortgage is way out there; so very rare
The government just doesn't seem to care

I don't think I'll dream of going back there
I've learnt a lot as life's gone on
I've made mistakes but I've also been fair
I know what they mean, when they say
Youth is wasted on the young

If only I knew then what I now know now
I never understood it then
But I do so know now
That's prophetic, that's poetic, how pathetic

But have you seen
The future children are changing
Gone the fast food way of behaving
It's the natural range they are now craving
No fats, no sugars; that's the new line
No smoking, no drinking
Well I must say it's about time
Yoga, Pilates Tai Chi and meditation
We are slowly becoming a healthier generation

And I have money in my pocket
My own little home, my own little place
I'm comfortable and warm
And content with my face

My husband is amazing
He adores me in every way
I look forward to our future
How many of us can say
I am so happy, so happy every single day

However this form I still don't like
To write it down to see it in black and white
I still feel anger and full of curses
I'll still jot down because I still feel I am

No matter how old I get
Just 49 and a little over ¾s

So do you see?
I'm determined not to agree
With what my birth certificate and life
Is trying to tell me

55! I DON'T BELIEVE IT

It came through the door
A sound I've heard a thousand times before
It fell from the letterbox to the floor
From today this memory will be there forever more

It wasn't a birthday card
It wasn't an invitation to a wedding
Or even a sad bereavement card

Maybe I've won a competition
The lottery or the football pools
Could this be a chance
A chance to get my share
After paying in all my dues

I tear the envelope open with some trepidation
And I reach deep inside
I don't believe it!
It was a card and it was an invitation
Informing and requesting my attendance
At the NHS clinic for my first
Bowel, testicular and prostate testing

Surely there must be some mistake
Surely my friends are having a jape
Has it come to the wrong kith and kin?
Could it be for my brother?
My Dad? Could it be him?
Someone else in the family tree
Anyone else I hoped, but not me

I look in the mirror
As I pass in the hall
I am shocked but I had to smile
I burst out in laughter
As looking back at me I see my father

My body seems displaced
Nothing is where it should appear
My luscious hair is shrinking back
It's now pocking straight out of my nose
And warming up the inside of my ears

My face is drooping
Everything hanging below
I've noticed a double, no a triple
No! I don't believe it, a quadruple chin
They quiver when the wind blows

Lines in my forehead
Dark bags under my eyes
Cheeks hang dog, so sad, so low
It can't be right, it can't be true
I don't understand the reflection
It must be lies, I just don't know

My barrel chest has become my barrel waist
My pectorals have shrunk
Of the muscle there is no trace
And my abs is disguised in soft disgrace

My arms and legs have become so thin
Like sticks stuck out of a rather large bin
My hips are aching, I have rickety knees
And I have found I have lost the ability to poo
And it burns like passing glass when I pee

I feel so crazed
I'm in such a daze
These are certainly not
My very best days

My fashion sense has left those oh so cool ways
When did my shopping change?
When did I get so disengaged?
I now specialise in off white shades of beige

My shirt is tucked into my shorts
I wear socks with sandals
Pulled up to my knees
I wear a belt AND braces
And a 70s blazer matched up to my jeans

I prefer slippers in front of the telly
Velcro on my shoes
And an elasticated cincture around my belly
A panama hat or a northern cap
A knotted hankie is always on tap
I don't exercise enough
I've become a slob, a couch potato
I only walk in the morning
To fetch the Sunday paper

I used to be a sports star
Captain of football and rugby teams
I ran the London marathon in my teens
I guess it stopped when I thought of other things
Like chasing lust and love and other dreams

The evidence continues as I try to emulate my son
With high fade hair
Low cut stretchy, ripped, skinny fade jeans
Brandishing Calvin Klein nickers
And a regretful tattoo I've inked on my bum

I bought an iPhone,
I tried social media
But it was embarrassing
Coping with text speak, emojis
And selfies with no face there

My friends and I hired some hogs
Harley Davidsons, well, of course
Illinois to California
We're heading west, coast to coast
Along route 66 no less

We've purchased all the necessities
We've bundled all the gear
Open chested leather jackets with extra paunch
And slicked back greasy, greyish hair

We've planned it for a while
Meticulous on all two thousand miles
With bright aspiring eyes
On our faces we bear a goofy smile

It's one last desperate adventure
One last middle aged affair
However when it comes to get up and go
Do we really dare?

Computers are taking over my mind
I feel I'm being left behind
For me it's becoming confusing
In this electronic gender world
I'm convinced I'm losing

It's all too late
I've resigned to my fate
I'm now harbouring a hernia
I'm afraid I'll develop dementia

I try to think back
When was the last time I went to a party?
When was the last time I went to a concert?
To a rave, a club, to a gig?
A chance to dance the night away

Coming round with a hangover
Sometime the next or the following day
When was the last time I didn't go home till morning?
Waking in a strange room in the dawning

When was the last time I woke in a strange bed?
A traffic cone upon my oh so sore head
When was the last time I did a line?
When was the last time I felt that fine?

Now I prefer a night in
Time in front of the telly
A bottle of water
An early night
A rich tea biscuit dipped in a mug of cocoa
I don't believe it! I've become so light

I look around at other men
Other men who've had it lucky
TV presenters with no hair loss
And have no belly

They look so perpetually young
It makes me question, what have I done wrong?
Do they have a youthful secret?
An elixir, a potion I haven't discovered yet?

No, but they have hair stylists and make-up artists
Personal trainers and teeth bleachers
It makes me sad to think of other fellas
I know it's only because I'm jealous

I worry about my loved ones
I'm concerned about my wife
Could be what I'm doing to myself
Cutting down my life?

I'll keep off all the take-aways
Start to count my calories
I'll keep an eye on what I eat
Prepare meals healthily seven times a week

I'll do a few press-ups
I'll take up running
Jump in a pool and begin some swimming
Instead of driving to work; as I like
Tomorrow I'll cycle; I'll take my bike

I'll give myself a shake
I'll write it up on a slate
As I've taken all I can take
I just hope it's not too late

I'm in a mid-life crisis, I recognise it now
I take a breath, I take a pause
I've started and got stuck
In the centre of the male menopause
But I've got to this age
And I count my blessings
I see what I've achieved and what I've got
I own a house on a large plot
I have kids that I adore
And a loving patient spouse

I understand and am grateful
I have no real worries
I have no real strife
What I crave for now
I had when I was young
That was a long time ago
That was another life

I look down at the children I've bred
I look down at the offspring that call me gramps
There it's been said
I look at how my life has been led

So what if I'm fifty five
I don't feel it in my head
I'm not on my knees
I'm not dead
In my brain I'm still young
In my heart I'm still twenty five

This card was just a warning ·
If I take heed and visit the consultant
And be on time at my appointment
Embarrassing though it might be

It will allow me to live an even longer life
Another fifty five years
Yes you heard
You just wait and see

RETIREMENT

It wasn't his idea
But after the complaining and moaning
And a lifetime of incessant groaning
I persuaded my dad it was healthier if he retired
I couldn't stand anymore
I was getting impatient and so extremely tired

I told him to put up his feet
Enjoy what's left of his time
Take stock of the years he has left
Was I being selfish or was it for the best?

I know he's not earning as much
But there are advantages enough
Cheaper car insurance
Cheaper life insurance

If he applies in a hurry
He'll receive a free ball point pen
And I've considered the family
I got him to pay out for a fully paid up funeral plan

We asked, where do you want to be put
When you are six feet under
In a church yard or a field
With a tree planted over?

In a wooden box or cremated?
Buried in a golden pot
No headstone to mark his stay
Only a flat etched silver plaque

He now qualifies for concessions
For travel, to the cinema
Or a night at the theatre
Cheaper meals in a café or the social club

I know he'd rather have concessions
On bottles of red and white wine
Cigarettes, carafes of brandy, cans of lager
And whiskey shots poured in a line

Magazines he's never seen before
Start falling heavily through the door
He's not ordered them
He's not paid for them

It seems they are free
It occurs because he's not that dim
That all of these companies
Are keeping a sharp eye on him

SAGA vacations we've heard
Can make you feel old and sad
But could they really be that bad
Bus trips and coach excursions

Circumnavigate the globe
With time to search, time to probe
I told him there was nothing finer
Than leaving port on an ocean liner

He seems to think I've lost my senses
As if he's become weak and defenceless
I gave him other magazines that promised much
To help make his life an easier touch

Everyday solutions around the home
Help in the kitchen, the garden
The bathroom, the bedroom
Jobs in the garage he can now perform on his own

I gave him membership to the National Trust
To visit museums and castles
Homes and gardens
Surely I hoped he would, please he must

I have considered it's time to exercise
Calisthenics to keep him fit and slim
A daily constitutional at the gym
A round of golf to walk a few miles
Fashion his swing and honing his style

But my dad's not so old
He's not so daft
This is to make my life not his
Less of a task
He said; if this is
What it means to not work anymore
If this is life when I'm forced to retire
He told me straight
You are a funny lad
But I'd rather carry on as I did before

FOR THOSE
WHO STOP AND THINK

DON'T LOOK AT ME......

Don't look at me; I know you're staring
The thoughts in your head are not always caring
You cross the street when you see us walking
To avoid the chance we may start talking

Those in wheelchairs and those that are blind
And those with health issues of any other kind
You move out of the way, you leave a wide berth
You think you're being useful
You imagine we don't mind

Do not patronise, don't be condescending
Do not treat us like we're frail
Do not treat us as a child
We may have a disability but we can still act wild

Communicate in a way you do everyone else
Don't try being too careful, it can seem quite false
We have our own thoughts, we have our own mind
Most of us work, we are all of one kind

We appreciate the help, but treat us with respect
It's not always needed, we don't always expect
Celebrate the difference
Do not show your prejudice
Or act out your blatant unwanted ignorance

We can all fit in
Just give us a chance
Don't be so polite around us
Don't lead us a merry dance

When young we were told we are special
We were told we are quite unique
But please try to treat us like others
Tell the world how we really think

THE LONELY SEAT

I see you looking at me, ignoring me
Going past without a care
I see you looking at me, ignoring me
With that baleful stare

I see you taking a look
Scrutinising as though perusing a book
You are in a bind I see, making up your mind
It's either me or the one behind

You leer then sneer and pass me by
I simply don't understand, I wish I knew why?
Please just tell me I implore with a sigh
You seem to ignore me. Oh I'm sorry are you shy?

Go on just for a second. Just have a go
I can't be that bad, you never know
I could be just what you are looking for
But you just bypass and walk out the door

Take a seat, have a pew, rest your bum
You must be tired, so please sit, come
Your legs are quaking, you must be sore
However you'd rather stand or sit on the floor

Am I worn, have my colours faded?
Do I have a rip, a tear? I feel so jaded
Am I soiled, am I wet? I don't feel it
Do I smell? I have no nose, I can't tell

Am I too large or am I too small?
I don't feel very different
Do I look infirm, too rickety?
I think you are just too nickety pernickety

You take one step, two steps
A glance, a little pause
One more step, then you've gone
Never to be seen anymore

I am just an empty seat
There's always at least one
I am anywhere, everywhere
We are an easy target, easy to shun

On a coach, a bus or a train
A private car or an aeroplane
In a restaurant, or a cinema
A coffee shop, a bistro or a theatre

"Excuse me, do you mind?"
"hello!, yes, who are you?
What do you want?
What can I do for you?
You want to sit?
No I don't think so

No you can't
I've changed my mind
I've revised
I don't think I like human kind"

Oh my God! I'm sorry, I won't complain
I think I'm claustrophobic
Oh my God! I can't explain, I apologise
I think I'm becoming xenophobic

You're squashing me and man you stink
I'm destined to be a lonely seat
NO! NO! please!
NO! you'll snap me, break me
Please somebody, somebody please

HELP ME!"

HOMELESS
(please give generously)

ASHORE

They waded through seas from a rickety boat
They tramped a most dangerous and perilous route
Having escaped from tyranny and persecution
Arriving on shore hoping for some conclusion

Stepping off a bus at Victoria station
Bedding down for the night in some confusion
Waiting for the promises that were made
Waiting for their inclusion, a chance to ply their trade

So, so many, a vast multitude
Travelling the globe, no voice spoken aloud
At the border no help, just checks
Immigrants and refugees alone on Trafalgar's steps

Hiding under bridges, cowering in doorways
Loved ones from villages, living on the streets
Trying to get undercover, to find some shelter
Trying to make their lives and families ends meet

They told them the streets were paved with gold
They told them the trees drip with money
They told them to let their dreams unfold
They didn't tell them the roads weren't milk and honey

They didn't tell them about the dirt and the grey
Owing thousands to traffickers, to come such a long way
They didn't tell them about the cold
They didn't tell them they may be sold

They didn't tell them they wouldn't be feeding
They didn't tell them they wouldn't be needing
They didn't tell them they had to beg for warmth
They didn't tell them their life had no worth

They didn't tell them what they should have known
Regret in hindsight with nothing shown
They wished for something a little more
They wished they hadn't come ashore

STREET

He was just a man
Wrapped up to the bone on the side of the street
Some would call him a tramp
Some would call him a layabout
A scrounger, some even a cheat
Lonely and forlorn in a coat of rags
And shoes two sizes too small
For his worn out feet
His day consists of working the pavement
A hound by his side his only companion
Feeding titbits from a burger
A kind soul has bought him
Sipping a lukewarm coffee
Someone else has bestowed him
He's been sitting all day
Curled up in the doorway
And as the dusk rolls in
And the light fades away
He pulls himself up
Checks everything's in order
Then moves away
Sometimes under cover
Somewhere a little quieter
Somewhere he hopes a little warmer

ABUSED

The arguments got too much
The abuse was ten times worse
An open hand, a closed fist
An unwanted touch, an expletive curse
Please don't tell your mum; our secret of course

No hobby horse, no dolls house
No hopscotch, no skipping ropes
No birthday treats, no Christmas bakes
Regretful friends lost forever
Closing down regretful hopes

This winter there is no family
This winters a Victorian bleak
This winter there is no home
This winter walking the empty streets
A blanket abandoned and worn
Gives no comfort, now all alone

In and out of hostels
Hidden in an alleyway
Under an embankment
Coddled by the bins
Forced heroin, pot and weed
Dope, grass, skunk and smoke
A pain of troubles aching within

This wasn't part of her future
This wasn't a fixture of her dreams
This wasn't growing up
This can't be what an adult means
A worse life she couldn't imagine
For a homeless girl of just fifteen

EVICTED

We're living in the car
Kids quiet on the back seat
The council housed us for a day, for a night
Anymore was classed as a treat

We'd got into debt
We'd got made redundant
Couldn't pay for all our food, cloths
Our housing, all our rent

We coped for a while
Being stringent, paying what we could
But the landlord was impatient
So the judges he then sent

In December we were evicted
We just took what was needed
Identification, medication, clothes
Our vehicle; still on loan

We took only what we could carry
Enough for a couple of days
Leaving our worldly possessions
We were heading for our graves

The snow is falling, the sleet is driving
The cold penetrates our bones
There's no real reason
Deep in this stark winter season

It shouldn't happen like this
There should be a better way
There should be somewhere else
Somewhere more comfortable for us to stay

ALONE

He's one amongst the forgotten
On the streets underground
There are others he won't talk to
So he keeps his head down

He resides amongst the filth and spoil
Bags, beer cans, cigarette butts and soil
Bottles, boxes and takeaway wrappers
Syringes and condoms from lusting matters

He lies beneath the clouds with no cover
He lives in the grey with no colour
His version of a soft duvet
And a warm pillow of feather

His neighbours are the creatures of the night
The crawling insects, the fleas, the lice
The rats, mice and clicking cockroaches
Stray dogs, abandoned cats and urbanised feral foxes

He loathes to graft, to beg, to ask for a penny
Because replies are shrift "we have not any"
But he'll not lose his dignity, he'll stay proud
He'll reply thank-you, god bless, have a good day
Determined, he'll refuse to be cowed

Sometimes he's amongst the low life that turn to crime
Thieves, pick pockets those that have done time
They think of nothing of attacking in an alley
For a phone, a purse, a couple of quid, some money

He drinks for sanity to make him forget
He smokes for warmth cadging as much as he can get
He's resisted the offer of meth and heroin
So tempting to escape into some kind of oblivion

On the worst days, when feeling down and distraught
He then considers sharing a squat
Breaking into derelict shops
Factories, empty houses and office blocks

Stay a few weeks, months, a little while
Then moving on a mile to the next available pile
His chances high of being caught and evicted
Thrown in jail and then rejected

He's done his dues, he's hit rock bottom
He can't see a way up, lost and down-trodden
He's tried to move on, to ask for charity
But he's found no empathy, there's little humanity

So, when the days over, he welcomes the night
Just a chance to sleep, to move from sight
As he slinks away, giving into fate
He dreams his hopes not wishing to wake

FOR THOSE LOVERS ARE WE

DEAR LONELY HEARTS STORE

Dear lonely hearts store

I'm not looking for a girlfriend at this moment if you please.

But I am looking for the companionship of a good woman, the company of a beautiful girl, the enticement of the opposite sex. The trust of a friend, a pal, a chum, a mate, somebody for my body, for my mind, for my soul, for my, well...... nuff sed.

I am looking for someone to go out with during the day, for coffee, for lunch, for strolling round the shops. I'm looking for someone to walk out with at night, for dinner, to the cinema, for a drink, to share some shots or maybe see a show or a concert, a gig, the theatre and then to wake up to in the morning; wishing I'd been near her.

But I'm not looking for a girlfriend at this moment if you please.

I am looking for someone that's comfortable in my presence and me comfortable in hers. I'm looking for someone to sit with in our pyjamas, in those awkward silent moments that don't actually seem awkward, just calm......as, to be able to hold her hand, maybe give a hug or a squeeze, even a cuddle with a kiss and a snuggle and hoping maybe, just for a moment, for us both to know we're not footloose and fancy free.

I am looking for someone to arouse all my senses, to see a twinkle in her eyes, to melt into her smile. To smell her perfume her most favourite scent. To hear her laughter, to sing her song, to touch her for a minute. Then make it clearer as we get a little nearer, for us both to know this is what was truly meant.

But you know I'm not looking for a girlfriend at this moment if you please.

I am looking for someone that nicks my food, picks the chips off my plate, snatches the chocolate from my hand, I'm looking for someone that will steal a kiss when my head turns around. To surprise me at the most unexpected moment, with a smack on my bum or a tickle in my tum…Ha Ha Ha stop it! When I really mean carry on.

I am searching for someone to share my thoughts and my feelings and my innermost secrets and to be able to share her ideas, her dreams, to journey where she wants to, to and fro. With her highs and her lows, experience all our peaks and our troughs, especially the peaks and the, er… bake-offs. SO LET'S GO GO GO.

But I'm pretty sure I'm not looking for a girlfriend at this moment if you please.

 I am looking to cook your favourite meal, whether stir-fry, chilli or KFC deal, or when you feel hung over, stressed and tight, a foot rub or massage will leave you so…blissfully right. Then run you a bubble bath with candles and oils, to ease your head, neck and shoulders, after your long working days and those long heavy toils.

I am hoping to share a bottle of wine or a tub of Ben & Jerrys when we are watching a DVD, a romance, a horror or something that's funny, or seeing a favourite sit-com on the TV and listening to albums and songs that we can both dance and sing along on the old MP3. A little piece of HIP HOP, a tiny bit of soul, some reggae, a touch of easy listening, a smidgen of R&B, a smack of rap and a lot of rock & roll.

Mmm, I may be changing my mind about not wanting a girlfriend at this moment if you please.

I'm hoping we'll join a gym, I'm hoping we'll go together, we'll try and keep slim, we'll feel so much better. Using all the machines, they've got the lot and if I do say so myself; we're gonna be

SSSIIIZZZLLLIIINNNGGG HOT

Then in the pool, we'll splash around, from front crawl, back stroke, butterfly and breast. We've got swim hats, arm bands, goggles and vest? Oh blest! You in your bikini with the long, long, long stroke, me in my mankini...HEYYY! I'm a proper, proper, proper bloke.

I am looking to go on a trip together, to ride on a train, a boat or a plane, to travel in a car, across the seas, across the skies to lands so afar. To explore vast monuments, the Taj Mahal, the Pyramids at Giza, the Great Barrier Reef. To be amid other cultures, to speak another language, to experience different beliefs.

Dear lonely hearts store

I'm getting so confused, do I really want a girlfriend at this moment if you please? Do I really want more?

I am hoping for someone that makes me smile, to share those funny moments, to share those sad moments, to laugh as well as to cry. I am hoping for someone, for someone to share our hearts on our sleeves together. I am hoping for someone, for someone to share our lives and to banish our loneliness forever.

Dear lonely hearts store

Am I looking for a girlfriend at this moment? As if...please, I don't think so, I'm meaning, well who knows? Ok, yes, definitely...I admit it, please, please?

Who am I looking for? I don't know, I'm not sure, do I have a favourite? A certain type? You could be blond or brunette, you could be red or pinstripe. You could be tall, you could be short. You could be well; dumb, you could be well; smart, just so long, whomever you are, you're still, well; sort of young at heart.

What should I call you? Should it be my sweetheart, my beloved, my heaven sent, yo my bangin' boo too, innit, my honey, me luvly, her indoors, the other half, my old lady, the missus? As long as when we part in the morning, we hug and kiss and promise to say we're gonna miss us.

Someone strong that can fend for herself. To be proud of you, to stick you high up on a shelf. Maybe I'm looking for the impossible when I decide to put you on a pedestal. With your feet on the ground but your head in the air, I really do, do care, someone that's a little bit nuts who likes, enjoys a person who's kind of a klutz. Someone that's rough and tough but also soft and stuff. Someone that needs me when the going gets too much

I know this is just a poem, a few characters in a script, a few words on a line, but maybe inside that's how I feel and if it is, I mean, man, than that's just fine. So if you like a good book, reading by the fire or skiing down a piste that started so much higher, then crashing into the bar, enjoying the atmosphere, hoping to get sloshed, drunk, tipsy or p p p p pissed. We could walk up Machu Pichu, or stroll up Kilimanjaro, maybe jump from a plane with hundreds of feet below you.

Aaaassshhhiiittte!!!

And if you could handle a dip in the cold English Channel or a soak in the warm Indian Ocean. If you enjoy a quick sunrise over the desert or the

slow sunset over the sea. If you do and I'm sure you do, then you could be the one, the one for me and me the one for you too.

Dear lonely hearts store

I am looking for someone at this moment, someone for friendship, someone for fun, someone maybe, just maybe, someone to spend a little more time in the sun.

MEETING MY WIFE

Well, I never, I did find someone, someone who cared, to celebrate birthdays and Christmas and all that I promised we shared. We've travelled the world, had some crazy times as a couple, we had many adventures, we lived as two in a bubble, then two became three and joy shone down on her and subsequently on me. Three becomes four and in the years to come who knows maybe even more. I find it extremely hard to compare the life I gained to the life I had once before. When I was single I hoped and I planned, as a couple I loved and felt grand, as a family that's when life really began.

Now it's fruit juice on the carpet, food scraps in the sink, watching a white wash tumble that includes a mysterious lone sock that's......pink! Toys in the living room, in the hallway on the stairs. Hardly what I'm used to it's quite a weird kind of affair. Dog forever barking, children screeching down the garden. When I was on my own, I never dreamed of this kind of burden. But now I have a love, a wife and a family to boots. I care for them all dearly, I've been able to put down some roots.

STRAIN & STRIFE

Of course as a precaution I need to warn you that it may not always sit as we want or travel with this favoured intention, it may not always go as

I planned or as I just mentioned. There may be dark days, there may be gloomy days and for both of us to agree; we like to think we will, but we may not always. However if we are careful we can use these times to learn and grow stronger, we can use these times to make our loving lives even longer. We will turn it around, we will turn over a new leaf. The hard times on this journey will not always be like this. We will forgive and we will forget and we will continue our lives together in pure and unabashed, unadulterated, immodest loving bliss.

Dear lonely hearts store

It's been a while since I wrote but I wanted to thank you, without you my life would have been broke. It's not been easy I grant you, crikey take note. For we are now responsible and we are learning to cope, as we look down on a few young someone's. Someone's to educate and someone's to feed someone's to inspire and someone's to lead. I trust they grow up to get girlfriends and boyfriends, I hope they grow up to continue the family tree. They may get it wrong, they may even blunder so I will set them as a parting gift your email address and mobile number. I know they will soon grow up and say goodbye. I know they will soon grow up leave the nest, spread their wings and fly away. You've done your job well, we'll appreciate and bow and let you continue as you may. Now it's time to love and be loved once more, for it had to be, that's just, you know, my girlfriend and me. And so as we walk out the door, we exit for the last time your useful, amazingly wonderful lonely hearts store.

A FRUITFUL LIFE

So as the years have rolled by, our hair has gone grey and we've got a little older. We look back at the magical, wonderful life we have led, we wish it could go on longer, but the days are getting shorter and as the world turns are minds are full of dread. But we look into our faces and at the lines our memories have created and that promise we made for so much more. We leave no regrets, we have no remorse, we've lived a long life, since we first met, in the lonely hearts store. Time now marches on and the last seconds go by, we vow to meet again, I tell you no lie. We touch and we see as we silently sigh, our last breath matching, our last tears catching as they drop from the corners of our eye.

PS. A NEW LIFE

So if you ever find yourself alone, thinking you always wanted to be on your own. Look deep in your heart, look a little further in your mind and it may be that you're not really sure about what you may need or what you may find. However don't snap and gripe and moan about wishing you now had more. Wake-up, get off the floor, take a walk, move out the door and you may find yourself outside your own real local

LONELY HEARTS STORE.

BLIND DATE

The bells and whistles of machinery
The bubbles of newly processed teas and coffees
The all night café groans in its popularity
Containing an average segment of humanity

The smells and sounds of regularity
A feeling of home and safe security
Sitting here waiting for a blind date
I'm taking a risk, I hope it will be fate

I saw her face on the internet
My emotions came as a crush
I'm glad it wasn't a live feed; only a photograph
It meant she couldn't see my blossoming blush

The seconds tick along, time on delay
Every minute seems like an hour
Every hour passes as a day
Patiently waiting for my future I pray

She will come I know, I say
I hope she's just late
Not changed her mind, not got lost
I trust she's not been led astray

I spy through the window
The fast footsteps that go by
None are slowing, not coming in
All passing quickly on their way

Then seeking the warmth from the remnants of my drink
My head starts to droop
The lids flutter over my eyes, my body stoops
I try to stay awake, to stay alert
I find I'm quickly starting to blink

And as the steam clouds the air
Through the smoky fragrant gleam
A sound punctuates softly
A voice invades my dream

Excuse me mate, are you awake?
Excuse me sir, I believe you're my date
Excuse me fool, are you there?
Well it's your loss mate
I'm outer here

I missed my chance
After falling asleep
In the oh so soft leather chair
Lol

LITTLE SOLDIERS

Give thanks to the innocents
Who shed blood sweat and tears
On churned farmers' fields
Where the wheat once grew

Give thanks to the children
Sent out to defend the ideals
So little did they know

Give thanks to the broken hearts
Of the families left behind
Believing in the price they paid

Who laughed, waved and cheered
As their kids were borne on ships
From the port to shores far away

Give thanks to those who returned
To live another day
And for those left behind
With nothing left to say

Give thanks to the mothers and fathers
Who cried on each other's shoulders
Mourning their brave little soldiers
Interred under poppies forever we will pray

MUM, WE REMEMBER

The flavoursome smells from the kitchen
Standing by the oven never far away
Baking for the WI and the rest of the family
You prepared the delicacies we all enjoyed
You nurtured our appetite
You stirred, you blended, you served
Then after we'd eaten
Weren't we well satisfied?

From French toast for breakfast
Sunday roasts for lunch
Steak & kidney, toad in the hole
Fish fingers, sausage and mash
Could it be for dinner
Or could it possibly be for brunch

Lets not forget the sweets and deserts
Baked rice pudding with the nutmeg top
Chocolate sponge and jam roly-poly
A big slice served straight from the pot
Enveloped with custards so golden
Then a slap on the wrist for licking the bowl
But worth it for the tasteful food so wholesome

Mum, we remember

The gardens you so enjoyed
The gardens you so loved
From the first break of dawn
With the early morning light
Through the afternoon to evening
At times you'd be there
Accompanied by the hoot of an owl
Beneath a celestial moonlit night

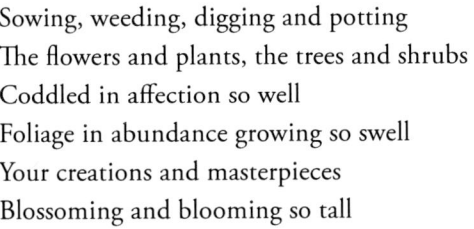

Sowing, weeding, digging and potting
The flowers and plants, the trees and shrubs
Coddled in affection so well
Foliage in abundance growing so swell
Your creations and masterpieces
Blossoming and blooming so tall

Mum, we remember

The rhythmic hum of the Singer sowing machine
Eagerly rattling off hobby horses
Teddies, dolls and soft toys
We always got so excited
Showing in our faces full of laughter full of joy

Cushions, curtains and pillow cases
Children's cloths and knitted jumpers
From patterns found behind the glass
On your ornate private bookcases

Mum, we remember
The Woman's institute
Participating with enthusiasm and fervour
A huge part of your heart, a big part of your play
Your moped piled high
With goods to sell on market day
At stalls, fairs and village fetes
All with happiness, all with clarity, all for charity

Behind the counter, behind the float
With a large bag of coins and the odd
(you've got to be kidding; I've no change for that
…fifty pound note)
Selling homemade handicrafts
Nic-nacs and keepsakes
Pastries, pies, tarts and cakes
Pickles, marmalades, curds and jams
And other simply great tasty bakes

Mum, we remember

Books that you were so fond and so proud
On display in glass cabinets
A collection, so colourful and neat
With some leather bound
Adventures set in boarding schools
Playing with Romany the dog

Adventures with the famous five
To classics Treasure Island, Count of Monte Cristo
Anne of Green Gables and Pollyanna
Poetically read the characters so real
So real, they came alive

Mum, we remember

Quite fondly, of those very, very early years
Of odd days out and weekly family holidays
Building sandcastles on the beach
Paddling to our waist in the frigid North sea
Sharing a bed in a typical
By the coast three room B&B

Or camping under canvas with the 6th Bury Scouts
With no real discernible toilet facilities
But we were having an adventure

We were having summer fun
We had no jobs to do
Apart from fetching water we had to use
And emptying out the dung from the camps
Many, many, many porta-loos

Yes we remember those very, very early years
Of odd days out and weekly family holidays
Yes...quite, quite fondly?

Mum, we remember

Your own little caravan
Your own special mini home from home
Somewhere you could be on your own
Somewhere you could find peace and solace
Amongst the materials that you owned
To locations you treasured
To places you chose to go

Along the lanes of the countryside
Tracks of the hills, by streams and brooks
Walking along the stony sea shore
You and your dog strolling together
Part of the scenery, part of you, forevermore

Mum, we remember

You were cook, you were gardener
You were nurse, you were poet and artist
And you were wife, mother and grandma
Bearing of loving daughters and sons
All distinct souls, all very different
But assuredly in truth a part of you in everyone
Granted you never favoured,
But you held a part in your heart
For all that you savoured

Now we all sit here in soft and silent contemplation
Reflecting on memories for us to recall
Ways of coping, a little deflection
We love you mum
We wish you well on your journey
We wish you well on your crossing
Back to nature, to your favourite garden you'll be
To find a place of hush
To find a place to reside
To find a place to rejoice
And a home for your spirit to be set free

Mum, we remember

Giving all with no tears, giving all with no fuss

Mum, we remember

Everything you ever did for us

MUM, WE REMEMBER

Thank-you mum

SHE WAS BORN A LITTLE GIRL

She was born a little girl
And that was enough for me
She came at five pm just after tea
A baby bundle
A swaddling in arms
Soap and talc and wrapped up warm
Sleeping, feeding, changing, screaming
Crying for no apparent reason
When her eyes were smiling
And mouth was gurgling
We loved it when she started laughing
For a short time there were disturbed nights
But now it's sorted, it's now alright
A year later she's just a dream
We're so connected
We've become quite a team
When she got to four
Her personality came to the fore
She's now caring and sharing
Counting sweets out on the floor
One for Toby, one for May
One for mum and one for Kay
Secondary school saw an intelligent soul
Ten going on twenty, growing tall
Like a sponge she's learning
Asking questions, forever yearning
I gritted my teeth and carried on bearing
Puberty was a time I didn't understand
She never listened, I was always banned
I was never right, I was always wrong
I hoped it was quick, not so long

Living through hissy fits extreme
Leaving childhood much too quick it seems
It was then that the girl in front I see
Is someone I recognise
She was becoming a mini me
I watched her grow and change
No two days were ever the same
Colouring her hair from short to long tresses
Changing from school uniform to party dresses
Bruised elbows, ragged knees
Thick jumpers and dungarees
Leather jacket and shorter skirts
Ripped up jeans and tie dyed shirts
Following fashionistas
Worrying about her finances
Dealing with her fears
Finding her place
Choosing her careers
I encouraged her lofty hopes
Saw how she learned to cope
Lived with her outrageous dreams
Communicating on teams
Shared in her happiness's
Watched over her illnesses
Now she's older becoming bolder
She still has tantrums
But not at me
It's at her partners, first one, then two, then three
At last we're pairing
She's very inspiring
Going on shopping trips
To swapping make-up tips
Planning a holiday with the gals

Taking a year out travelling the world
Living her own life
Ruminating on becoming a wife
Turning from fairy princess to royal queen
Now she's having a little girl
And that's enough for me

ANGELS

Do you believe in angels?
I'm always being asked
Do you believe in the celestial body?
Dropped from heaven to perform such miraculous tasks
Do you believe in a winged seraph in human form?
That wrap their wings around you
To protect and keep you warm
Do you believe in their perfect nature?
Whose beauty masks an ugly world
Where one look will transfix
And make us feel unconcerned
Do you believe in the energy of halos?
Surrounding their spiritual heads
And the forgiveness they weald
Or so it's always said
Do you believe in their purity and kindliness?
That seem so hard to deny
And the goodness, selflessness and charity
Or do you believe it's lies?
Do you believe in angels?
I'm always being asked
Do I believe in pixies and elves, hobgoblins and trolls?
I've always replied NO!

Why can't they let it go?
But just last week I changed my mind
I do believe in angels
Since the one I met is you.
You make my life complete
You make my knees go weak
I look forward to seeing your smile
Every morning when we awake
You even share my lifelong love for lemon drizzle cake
You cheer me up. I'm never blue
Why you chose me?
I didn't have a clue
Your rectitude was beyond me
But it's the truth I now see
I love everything about you
More than I love a cup of tea
I love your eyes and the rest of your face
I adore the fringe in your hair
I admire the way you sit in a chair
When you walk with me down the street
Where once I was so rude to everyone I meet
I now so happily greet
I've changed for the better
I'm no longer sour and bitter
Your virtue on my soul
Has pieced me together
You've made me whole
I still don't really understand why you are here
But through this world I no longer have fear
There are lots I haven't said
However the list is long, it'll never be read
I do believe in angels I now say
I trust everyone does
I romantically pray

FOR THOSE PASSING
THE MIDDLE

WHAT'S A RETREAT?

The whine of a bullet from muskets shot
The crash of the cannon through debris hot
Choking cloud of dust and smoke
Swallowing blood and sweat
Impenetrable sound, impenetrable throat
Men screaming and crying
On quagmire sand, cemented there dying

Young bandsman down espy command
Rises on knees unsteady and quaking
Up aloft albeit the foe
Up aloft albeit the shaking
Unshoulders bugle from his jacket
Lips embouchure emits the sound of sunset
Defiance of crowd, defiance of racket

Retreat, retreat sound the retreat
Come away from the noise
Come away from the bluster
Behind the lines the troops do muster

A spa break or holistic centre
Feeling enriched with upper class splendour
Expansive grounds
Manicured lawns
Such unwonted refined
Such a wonder
Snuggled abound in gowns and slippers
Set facials and wraps
Skin and muscles pummelled
Hair coiffured, then coloured
Nails cut then filed

Ensconced in bubbles of perfumed oils
Relaxing head neck and shoulders
After long working days
And longer arduous toils
Backache, headache, stressed and tight
A foot rub or massage will leave you oh so, so
Blissfully......right

Retreat, retreat sound the retreat
Come away from the noise
Come away from the bluster
Behind the salon the serene will muster

A place of study, a place of learning
A new year, a new season
With eager students come a yearning
Through hallowed grounds
Through college halls of ivy
For a week residential
Or a day spent only

Arts and craft or basket weaving
Photography, calligraphy
After dinner speaking
Tutored a new language
French, German, Cantonese
Russian or Norwegian
The world is yours for the taking
Be sure to take it whatever your leaning

Retreat, retreat sound the retreat
Come away from the noise
Come away from the bluster
Behind the chalk, the educated will muster

A Buddhist temple high in the mountains
Where the red sun sets
Aloft in the clouds of Bhutan, China, India, Tibet
A place to go for divination
To practice yoga, tai chi or meditation
An experience just once
Or a lifetime of growth
A life of learning and satisfaction for most
A silent retreat, no noise to hear
Listen to the peace, to have no fear

Learn to accept your own lone mind
Learn and listen to others you'll find
From small beginnings you'll grow
Finding acceptance through time will follow
From apprenticeship to ordination
Progress on the celestial path of Buddhism
To a teacher of religious sanctification

Retreat, retreat, sound the retreat
Come away from the noise
Come away from the bluster
Behind the precepts the divine will muster

Home is my sanctuary
Somewhere I can be alone
Somewhere I can find peace and solace
Amidst the materials that I own
Regard the TV; channels that keep me tethered
Hearken to music; my guilty secret pleasured
Prepare the delicacies that I enjoy
Nurture my appetite
To blend, to serve well satisfied

Lock the door, draw close the curtains
Away from prying eyes
Of which I can be certain
Walk around with no pretension
In the house I built
In the home I rendered
Somewhere I can be true to myself
Away from life's constraints; to be free
Somewhere I can, simply just…be

Retreat, retreat, sound the retreat
Come away from the noise
Come away from the bluster
Behind the walls I will muster
Now that's a retreat

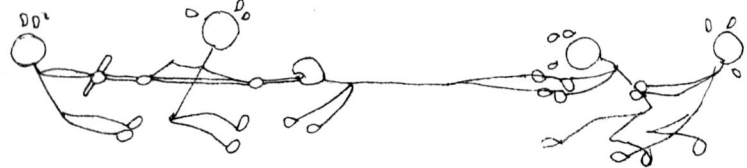

THE ICE LICKER

As a child I accidently on purpose licked a pipe covered in ice.
I was overly curious. It looked so tasty, it seemed extremely nice, I tried
to lick it twice. But after the first time it got stuck to my tongue. I tried
to pull it off but it couldn't be done. No matter how hard I tugged it
wasn't enough. It seemed so silly, it was completely daft, I panicked and
blushed and squeaked out a nervous laugh. I called for my mum but my
words wouldn't come. I mumbled and gargled my tongue felt so numb. She
couldn't understand so I pulled on her hand and when she turned round
she said a little offhand.

"Oh my God my boy, what have you done? Is that a pipe stuck to your
tongue?"

I couldn't reply so I nodded my head, she looked so scared I thought I
was dead.

"right then boy, let's see what we can do".

I wished she'd hurry, I was now desperate for the loo.

She placed one hand on my forehead the other held the pipe, she pushed
and pulled with all of her might. After a while she said.

"it's no good, it won't come loose, this pipe on your tongue is just too
tight. We'll call your father with his rugby team they'll have the strength to
pull it off clean".

When they arrived they stood in two lines, half grabbed the pipe, half
held my legs.

"this should work" they remarked with some positive hope.

When they took hold they pulled as if I was a rope, it hurt so much
I begged them to stop, but they didn't understand they thought I could

cope. They then pulled much harder and then even faster, I'm sure I could feel my tongue and my legs getting longer and larger. With a one, two and three, one side heaved the other side hauled, the sweat on their face broke out and started to pall. They grunted and groaned, gasped and moaned, when all of a sudden they all collapsed to the ground, with splutters and coughs all of these muscular men ran out of puff.

My mum said, "the fire brigade. Why on earth didn't I think of them before?"

I gargled in response "I'm really not sure?"

When they came in their big red machine, they had all the gadgets it seemed like a dream,

"come on men let's ease it off, this'll be easy lads, lets prise it off"

With hydraulic machines and steam laden jacks they tried to lever it off. When they started them up the noise was so loud, the steam formed a cloud, the vibrations ran through the ground. And just for a moment there I thought it was loosening but I actually found it was really only bruising. In the end it proved no good, the hydraulic machines all broke down, snap went the jacks and all those brave firemen, well they were useless, they all got the sack.

By this time my bladder was screaming, it was the lavatory that I was desperately needing.

My mum decided to take me to my school, with all the teachers brains they should know what to do. They found an empty classroom where they held a meeting. The teachers, professors and scientists went over the problem. It seemed very fleeting. The gathering was over so very fast, I don't think they gave it much of a chance. Then they decided almost together.

"I'm sorry my lad we can't think of anything better, I'm afraid there's nothing we can do; we worked out all the equations, measured the calculations, thought of the physics tried the biology but the theories not just, I'm afraid the answers not with us". We were so disappointed as we left the playground behind.

"let's go somewhere else and see what else we can find"

We decided to visit the hospital because it's where we were led, I know it's not the same but Doctors are good at getting pots and pans off children's heads. We went to see if they had a spare bed. The consultants, nurses and students all stood around. They measured my pulse, they listened to my chest, they took my temperature, they turned me this way and that way and I ended up upside down. It was very embarrassing as they prodded and probed and stood there discussing. However again there was no help, no relief, nothing any one could do, no tablets, syrups, pills or potions would assist, they had no clue.

"there's nothing I'm afraid that will work for you".

As they moved off continually chatting, rubbing their head, picking their nose and scratching their bum, they walked down the corridor and declared they were done. By the time we left the hospital it was late in the morning, everyone had heard, a crowd was forming.

"Oyez, Oyez, Oyez" shouted the town crier "everyone gather and see the boy with a pipe stuck firmly to his tongue. There'll be food and drinks, singing and dancing, we'll all have a laugh, we'll all have some fun".

People started to surround us, quick as you like, they came by coach, by car, lorry and bike. Newspaper journalists and TV reporters turned up in the crush, they all came in a big red BBC bus. They took photos, they filmed us, some with microphones were there to interview us. I just thought why are all of these people making such a fuss? The council then took control, it was such a relief. They set up barriers and lights to protect mum and me. It had to do with something they called health and safety. I understood when they said the armed forces were coming.

But before they did I tried to let them know that my stomach was cramping, my bladder was bursting but nobody was listening. They were all so busy ignoring.

The Airforce were summoned, the Navy were bidden, the Army

requested 10.000 troops all sent out in camouflage and hidden. They all marched toward us across the icy ground, all in their uniforms, all feeling proud. They had many opinions.

A private suggested, "why don't we cut it off".

A sergeant had an idea, "why don't we shoot it off".

A captain remarked, "why don't we blow it off"

The Commanding Officer listened to everything he heard. he very politely answered, "very good suggestions men but all so dumb and all so absurd".

Then out of nowhere we were handed an invitation. After we read it we were struck with elation. We were invited by the government to 10 Downing Street, as the Prime Minister had heard and she wanted to meet. We were escorted by the police in a black limousine and deposited outside the famous black door. Once inside we were taken down a hall, through to an office, so plush it had polished mahogany floors. There was the Prime Minister behind a large desk, seated in a very large chair. She shuffled some documents, signed some papers, then when she looked up, she said

"well hello there"

She looked me up and down with a critical eye, she asked me what was wrong, my goodness was she blind. I told her as best I could what had happened and what had been done. When she replied she spoke like my mum.

"well my boy, it seems you've gone through; ideas and suggestions both old and new. All I can suggest; is if through the winter the pipe is still stuck to your tongue, you'll have to wait for summer, when if you are lucky the ice will melt in the sun. However in the meantime there's something else that must be done".

A new law was suggested, it was very quick for its type. It was proposed on a Monday, written on a Tuesday and passed on a Wednesday. From now on you will be arrested and thrown in jail for licking ice off a pipe. Before we left I asked for an autograph and a selfie. Me, mum and the Prime Minister bunched up together with faces all smiley. There was just one more favour I needed to ask, I knew I had to hurry I knew I couldn't last.

"excuse me Mrs Prime Minister, do you mind if I used your toilet, I've been waiting all day and I really can't hold it".

She replied, "of course my boy, that would be fine, it's just down the hall, the last room at the end of the line".

I pushed the door open and went inside, it was quite amazing the best loo I'd seen in all of my time. There was a marble sink, toilet and floor, there was a heavy gilt mirror hanging behind the back of the door. The toilet paper had the face of the Queen, imagine wiping your bottom with the portrait of the Queen, it really was very obscene. All of the taps, chains and levers were made of pure gold. They looked like antiques, so very, very old. The towels felt so soft of which there were a few and like at home there was a match to light to disguise the smell of poo. There were bottles of perfume, liniments and oils to freshen yourselves up and paint all your nails. I placed my feet in front of the loo and started to wee. It had been so long it came out in a rush. It bounced off the walls, it flew through the air, splashed on my face and landed in my hair. It slowly slipped past my eyes, dripped off my nose and dropped on my tongue. It felt so gross as it was done. I licked my lips and then realised the pipe on my tongue had fallen into the pan. Was I free, really, oh man. I was so happy I ran round the bathroom and cried out yippee. The warm wee on my tongue had melted the ice. I looked in the mirror just to make sure, the pipe that was there, was there no more.

The morale of this tale if there is one at all, if you see something tasty and extremely nice, do not take a lick, not ever once and certainly not twice

A BLISTER ON MY THUMB

I was swinging with a hammer
Causing quite a clamour
When my son shouted out "DAD, ARE YOU DONE?"
That's when I missed the nail in the wood
And instead, hit the nail on my thumb

So there I was waiting in A&E
Not having a lot of fun
Patiently queuing for the nurses to come
And treat a huge blood blister
I've created on the end of my thumb

I know it doesn't sound much
It's not a broken bone, a head injury
Or even a hernia in my tum
But to me it's really important
This blister on the end of my thumb

I'm hoping to get it lanced
I'm hoping it won't hurt
But I've researched on the internet
And it says it may be painful
Cause an infection and create a mite spurt

I thought about doing it myself
Fixing it at home, popping with a needle
But my wife wasn't really keen
She thought it would cause a mess
And get blood on the dining room table

The next patient arrives
Then two, three and four
And before very long there are twenty
Then even more

The waiting room is filling
We are running out of seats
I'm surrounded by people
All walking off the streets

I've been waiting for a while
To get my blister done
We don't seem to be moving
What on earth is going on?

Everyone has noticed the growing blister on my thumb
It's expanding every second, stretching, increasing
Watching it quite intently
It's now the size of my bum

There' a throbbing in my hand
There's a pounding in my head
My heart is racing faster
I'm starting to feel the panic

Starting to feel the dread
If I don't get rid of this blister soon
I'm afraid I'll drop down......

DEAD!!!

More people are pouring in
It seems the word has spread
Selfies are being taken
Journalists are asking questions
I'm now being featured on the telly
HEY! Part of the news at ten

We are keeping an eye on the blister on my thumb
It's taken on a life of its own, I know it's not done
The blood is pumping, veins are popping
I swear I can hear it squeak, shriek
Gasp, groan and moan

We all watch it getting bigger
We all watch it getting worse
If the nurses don't get a move on
I'm afraid it's going to......

(BANG!!!)

Burst

There was a humungous explosion
The contents flew through the air
Covering the walls, the ceiling, the floor
And all of the tables, magazines, newspapers and chairs
I knew it was going to happen
It got to an extraordinary size
But now that it's gone, I look at my thumb
And feel quite relieved
As there's nothing much there
Only a little patch left; besides

The doctor appears for the first time and says
"sir, I'm glad your thumb is better and the blisters gone
But I think you'd better leave
I think it's time you should move on"

I didn't understand
Until I saw all the other patients
All standing and watching me
With angry looks upon their faces

The crowd are dishevelled, drippy and dirty
The receptionist and nurses are too
All covered in a slimy mixture
Of red blood, yellow pus and sticky goo

It dropped off their hair
Dripped off their nose

Ran down their cloths
Even squelched in their shoes

I saw eyes of confusion
Some looking sour and bitter
But it really wasn't my fault; I try to explain
If only the doctors were a little bit quicker

But the look upon their faces
Tells me this isn't going to be good
I'm surrounded on all sides in a temper
Everyone is fuming, shouting and screaming
If only I hadn't come as my wife insisted I should

I felt sick with regret and queasy with remorse
Taking a frightened step back
I went crashing to the floor
Slithering and sliding in the mess
The grunge, the grime and the gore

Then I had an idea, I'd thought of a plan
A way to make a sneaky escape
To get away from all of these people
The poor victims of my mistake

So I went swishing around the legs
And slinking between the shoes
Despite the pains, aches, and sores
Carefully I made my way to freedom
Quietly I exited through the double doors

I promise from now on when attempting DIY
And swinging with a hammer
I'll keep an eye on what's to be done
I'll try and aim better and hit the nail in the wood
And not the nail on my thumb

TATTOO

Like collections on a window sill
Imprinted and so thin
They seem so real and as much of a deal
And just so very still

A tale of magnificence ready to be told
A memory of events past
As a decoration
Of history gone cold

Of feelings and emotions riven of heart at a time
A way of leaving a positive sign
Some later on may be full of regret
Some are reminders of relationships once wept

Some are written
As letters of poetry and prose
Or copies from a book
That someone else chose

Pictures anointed in black and white
Others may be duller, as greys of light
An eclectic mix of extraordinary hues
Greens, reds, purples, oranges, yellows and blues

Some vast in their making, so painful whilst taking
Others so small but of no less a partaking
The name of a child or a loved one
A single heart breaking

A way of showing character and personality
Announcing to the world
Look at me, here I am
This is who I am, actually

A way of hiding or disguising who you really are
A wanting or craving for those near and those very far
Or letting out your frustrations from within
So quiet, not shouting, never a noise and hardly a din

Some so hidden
No one knows they are there
Just something so personal
That you hold so close, so dear

No reason for this use of pen and ink?
It's something that took your fancy
Something you well just like
You think

And for all those people you see abound
Strangers smiling and laughing
Heads shaking or nodding
There's an affection from all of those around

A whole life's saga
Not with words on paper, but tales no less
A profound moment of art
With no hesitation I guess

Quick on the draw, on a coin flip with a dime
After a drink, a drunken moment to shine
Or a slow thought, sought for a while
Shame to make a mistake, if it's not your style

Is it not quite right, a little oft centre
Where a sleight of hand will correct
Adding much to the pleasure
Never to be taken away, a story to treasure

From the top of your head
To the soles of your toes
A journey so languid
A liquid of prayer, a mark to pose

Sinuous through curves
Forms and recesses
Beneath your cloths
Jackets, trousers and dresses

Whether you love them or whether you loathe them
Whether easy seen or just a peep
To the beholder its something said and bold
On something that's just skin deep

HOME FROM HOME RULES

For your stay here I welcome all
I'll provide warmth and comfort
From bedroom to kitchen, bathroom to hall
You are welcome to make yourself at home
I only have seven requests as a rule

If having friends and family around to play
Be mindful of others, keep the noise down
Announce the visitation and not too long a stay

Turn off lights when not in a room
This will turn down the landlords
Noise and annoyance to a low boom

When charging computers, phones, i-pads and hoovers
Turn off at the plug when finished, don't be lax
Or an extra charge for electric may have to be taxed

Be careful of anything that's been lent
Breakages may have to be paid
As they are not part of the rent

Leaving the house for the day
Lock the door and look after the key
Try not to lose it or lend it to anyone else
To help guard against theft and burglary

The partaking of drugs and smoking I will not allow
But a spot in the garden I will for now

When departing at the end of your stay
Only take what's yours
Tidy the room as you found it
It's only curtesy don't be slack
I thank you in advance, I hope you enjoyed it
You never know, I might allow you back

Keep to these small rules your stay here will be a breeze
If not I have to warn you, you may be asked to leave

THE MANAGERS ARE WITCHES

Their lair is locked in a secret place
Where spells are sought
Planned and placed
Voices whispered beyond the wood
Incantations and hexes
Up to no good
If you are invited in
Don't raise your head
Don't lift it high
Do the sign of the cross
Don't dare say hi
The managers are witches
Of that there is no doubt
You never see them
You never hear them
You're so blind when they're walking about
Beware when seeming tender
As trusting is never the answer
They are masking their true self
So take extra care
It may be a hindrance to your health
Once lured in try not to acknowledge
Don't stare in their evil eye
You'll feel in a trance
And heave a heavy sigh
Once under their spell
You may be sent to the deepest darkest pits of hell
However one day they'll be unearthed
Then god and heaven help them
Through fire and brimstone fast
To purgatory and perdition they will be cast

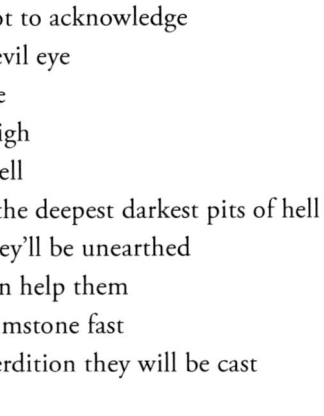

YOU'LL NEVER FORGET YOUR HAT

When departing a house
Exiting a restaurant, a shop or a bar
Eliciting from a train, a plane
A bus or a car

You'll never forget your hat

The usual items you accidently leave
Mobile phone, glasses, bag, your keys
Items such as that
But I tell you now quite honestly

You'll never forget your hat

Your wallet you may have left back
Your watch, a pair of gloves, your scarf
Your umbrella left on a rack
But I do insist and I'll continue to tell you

You'll never forget your hat

And everything else of like kind
Whenever you've walked out
From friends, family, loved ones, their homes
With other thoughts that fill your mind

Like past mistakes, future plans
Your wishes and hopes
Strawberries and cream
Your nightmares and dreams

It might never cross your mind
When you leave these behind
But I guarantee, it's such a fact
You'll never ever, no really not ever

You'll never forget your hat

I'll continue to remind you
When you leave a place of warmth
Where you've sat by the glow of a hearth
You step outside as the rain patters your bald pate
The breeze kisses with a chilly touch

It's just enough, a subtle reminder
Like a light touch on your shoulder
When the heat escapes from your scalp
You feel the cold and the damp

Then you'll always return and go back

To pick it up, as

You'll never forget your hat

Now where did I put my coat?

SOCIAL MAN

I wish I was a social man
I'd have more fun as part of a clan
However I find it hard to converse in a group
My throat closes up like a child with croup
I try to join clubs and meets
But my shyness I find so hard to beat
I try my best, I try to jest
I try to laugh off my fears
It's better than starting with the tears
I stay for one week maybe two
Then I'll make an excuse
I'll cry off with the flu
If I get invited to a wedding, a funeral or party plans
I'll be found in the kitchen washing the pots and pans
And if someone begins to try some flirting
I'll hide behind some full length curtains

This all sends a shiver through my heart
Even entering the doors
I find hard to start
I'm ok on a one to one

Anymore just can't be done
I'll try to be social man
But really I'm not much of a fan
If I go to a club or down the pub
To gain some courage I'll have a drink
But I never know what to say
My brain always forgets how to think
I'm not a very social man
I can't do chit chat like most people can
I can't just sit and talk
I find it too much hard work
So through the exit I'll walk
I'd rather go home
Be on my own and sit in the dark
I've come to accept the way I am
However I wish I was a social man

ONE FOR THE ROAD

Do you remember those games we played as a child
Some were quite tame, others exceedingly wild
Like pin the tail on the donkey
Musical chairs, freeze tag outside
Though not always fair
Hide and seek
Where my brother used to cheat
At school we skipped along a touch
Playing hop scotch and double dutch
I was a great fan of kick the can
And capture the flag wasn't so bad
However the best games all told
And I'm sure you'll agree
Were the ones in the car
The ones for the road
Like I spy with my little eye
Twenty questions, hangman
And cows on my side
But the one my sister liked best
Was her version of bingo scavenger quest
But instead of counting cars or animals in a field
She liked spotting road kill on the motorway
That was her ideal
Though our parents weren't keen on this particular venture
We'd get points for each and every dead creature
Rats, bats or mice gained one
Two for birds squashed along the kerbs
Hedgehogs neatly flat were next with a three
Or a four with it's quills stuck firmly to the floor
Five for a rabbit or a hare
More with no fur, just bare

A squirrel was a six because they're very quick
So much harder to hit
You'd get seven if you're lucky
Which is loads for frogs or toads
Eight for stray dogs
Nine for abandoned cats
The same for urbanised feral foxes
Often foraging in old cardboard boxes
But the biggest earner was a badger
They were given a ten
Because they were so big
We always thought they must weigh half a ton
We don't play these games anymore
Because of course we're adults now
We're no longer four
And as parents ourselves we wouldn't approve
Not anymore
But our children of today
No longer want to play
As they have lap tops, mobiles and consuls
To keep them busy as the journey whiles away
Probably just as well
And they do seem to keep them quiet
They never get bored or fed up
Or continually ask
Are we there yet?
Although sometimes looking back
As siblings often do
We catch ourselves when we say
We wish we could have one more game
Just one more play
Just one more for the road

MOVING

The rug is gathered up
Sliding from the hall
Vanishing through the front door
The living room is empty
As it was once before
Shelves have packed up and gone
The sofa, the armchair, the ottoman, stool
Pictures loosing off the wall
Following each other
Antiques? We haven't a clue
The TV went
The gramophone too
The kitchen devoid of white
The bedroom furniture gone
It's now so light
The boxes are packed with all we've got
Now stacked in the corridor
That's your lot
And after the encore when the curtains have dropped
And the stage is clear
Finally it's over
We've made our move
Thank goodness my dear

FOR THOSE WHO LIKE
TO RANT AND RAVE

Here's a question. Do you ever get frustrated, annoyed or upset, do you ever get tired, impatient or angry about life around you. What goes on in your home or work or just the environment you live. Are there things that are out of your control, how people affect others by the acts they perform or the words they've said. How some don't follow the rules or the rules themselves not making much sense. Where just a slight change would make things better. Think before you talk, give thought for others around you. How what you do may affect your family, your friends or neighbours. Here's a chapter about the little things, the large things that can annoy, some just for a second, others may last all day. I call them blind rants and I know we all like to complain. Here are just a few, if you have others I would love to hear from you. Please get in touch.

TALKING

Why do people talk in doorways?
Can't they see they're thoroughfares and walkways?
Why do people nitter natter, chitter chatter
Where other persons are trying to get through?
Stopping others getting on with their day

In the way, causing affray
Blathering, you can't just stand and stay
You don't seem to understand
You're being quite crass
Not allowing anyone else to pass

Why can't you meet in a pub?
In a café? In the local park?
Arrange a time in your own house
A cup of tea, a cake

Somewhere with a little more class
A picnic amongst the long grass
Is it too much to ask?
Should there be lay-bys dotted along the path?

PARKING

Why is it that able bodied people
Park in disabled bodies slots?
They are there for those with a reason
Those with a blue pass for the season

Why can't you walk a few more paces
Park at other allocated places?
Is it that you don't care or are you too lazy?
Could your sense of right or wrong be going hazy?

SHOPPING

Why is it that some people
Are just not ready to pay at the checkout?
When doing a weekly shop
They've had plenty of time as they say
Oh! Sorry I forgot

As they rummage in their bags
And dig deep in their pockets
Oh! And I've got these coupons
And do you mind if I give you my change
Coppers instead, to make up a pound?

And the chatter they make seem so inane
And all you want is someone to blame
However try to think of others before yourself
All this ranting is not good for your health

So try not to get annoyed
How else are you going to be employed?
Just wait and listen
Their repartee you may enjoy
Let them take their time
You are the one that's next in line

SPEAKING

I'm always being accused of mumbling when I speak
Of not enunciating words clearly
Not loud enough to be heard
And just a whisper or a squeak
When I'm asking questions or giving answers
I try to talk so my instructions are understood
But I know it's frustrating when you need a repeat
What was that?
Pardon?
Excuse me?
Maybe I should write it down in a little note book

MANNERS

What's gone wrong with peoples manners?
No please, no thank you
No letting you go first
No offering a seat to the infirm
Or a mum who's pregnant

Please let others take a pew and sit down
Being polite costs nothing
So prove to your Gran when she insists
You're really quite a nice young man

SALESPEOPLE

Why do cold callers
Ring us 10.000 times a day?
When they come round they insist
They demand. They persist
Once in a lifetime they say

They want you to pay
You tell them to go
You're not interested
You can't afford to buy
Please, you try to insist
I don't want you to stay

They persuade, they assure
They brainwash
They've done it all before
You become tired and confused
You end up signing they say you can't lose

You felt pressured
You felt badgered
You didn't know what to do
You just wanted them to leave
It's your house, your home so please just go

But once they've gone
You know you've been fooled
You feel ripped off, you feel rung dry
They made you feel ashamed and angered
Now it's time to call trading standards

COUNCIL

Why can't the council repair
Paths and sidewalks?
They always work on the roads
Which is all well and good

But what about the vulnerable people
Unsure on their feet
Pushing prams
Pulling cases and trollies
Surely they could

Ankles turned or broken
Knees grazed or popping
There are pits and depressions
Where slabs are turned and risen

Tarmac and concrete torn and rotten
Not a welcoming sight
For any visitors coming
Leaving a really bad impression

RUBBISH

Why do people throw away rubbish
Next to bins they pass when walking by?
There are cigarette butts, chewing gum
Then there's crisp packets and
Take-away wrappers
Take it home
Why can't they give it a try?
Litter thrown from cars
Buses and truckers
Filling the roads, blocking the gutters
Tin cans, cardboard, plastic bottles and glass
Piling up on the manicured grass
Then there are those that fly-tip
Not using the councils dumps
Turning beautiful nature
Into dirty and ugly clumps
With building waste of
Lumber, bricks, mortar and rubble
Pipes and debris of scrap metal
Household white goods of fridges and freezers
Ovens, washers, dryers and cupboards
If only they could be careful and mindful of others

TRAINS

Why aren't there enough carriages
On trains for those who've bought a ticket for a seat?
We should bring back third class travel
Stick us in a cattle truck

It's wouldn't be great
But it would be cheap
It's better than having to stand
Nowhere to put your bags
Your bike or your pram

Can't grab a drink
When the trolley comes round
Pushed and pulled
This way and that

Tripping over luggage
Losing your balance
It's hard work to keep your stance
Please let us in first class

Where the seats are empty
Please we don't ask for much
We don't need a lot
Adding more coaches would be a nice touch

COFFEE SHOPS

Why is it that baristas wrap the cord of a teabag
Tightly around the handle of a cup?
It may be ok if you want your drink so strong
You can stand the teaspoon up
But I like to drink it weaker and thinner
Not slurp it darker and thicker

And what is it when they put a napkin
Under your cake on a plate?
Prising it off leaves tissues on the base
You don't want to be fiddling with sticky fingers
Getting most of it on your cloths
And the rest of it on your face

And why can't there be two aisles?
One for those new-fangled
Expensive, amazingly super fantastic
Noisy ear popping, steam laden pings and bells
Take an age double espressos, cappuccinos
Mochas, affogatos, flat whites, lattes and café au lait
And one for those who just want a simple
Thirst quenching, relaxing afternoon cup of tea

MOBILE PHONES

Why is it that people on mobiles
Are so slow and just dawdle along?
Walking along the path
Not concentrating amongst the throng
Head bowed down not looking where they're going
Or where they've come from
Then suddenly with no warning
We certainly didn't see it coming
Stop in the middle of the pavement
So we nearly have an accident
As we smack into their back
With no time to slow down
Or swerve and go around
If only they gave it some thought
But we all know it's the basic caring that they lack

POLITICIANS

How is it that you politicians can make yourselves look silly
When invited to appear on the telly?
Be proud and privileged to be a guest on the show
Show off your university education
Use the power of your elocution
But do you ever answer the questions?
No; I don't think so
Try not to go off on a tangent
Talking about another subject
Don't try to be on the defence
Sitting precariously on the fence
You are being inconclusive
So innocuous as you mumble out a reply
We know you can't tell the truth
But try to avoid telling a lie
You attempt a different tack
As the interviewer gets back on track
You try to be devious and slippery
So never answer back
You begin to look uncomfortable
As your cheeks start to blush
As you lose your decorum shouting in a rush
Trying to come back with a rejoinder
You want to run not loiter
You wished you hadn't appeared
You wished you weren't there
This conversational exchange
Has now turned strained so very strange
The query is echoed
The presenter won't let it go
Please god. Just let me run home

The continuing replication
Is becoming an interrogation
You start to pray for some salvation
I sometimes feel sorry for the member of parliament
I often wonder why they are there?
They may as well have had a mannequin
Sitting in that chair
Isn't it time we had an honest lord or member
To tell us the truth?
To tell us what we really want to know
Instead of spouting out such gobbly-goop

ON A MORE PERSONAL NOTE...?

When I first met you
Those simple things I found so cute
Like rolling your eyes
And clearing your throat
I now find so annoying
I'm no longer enjoying
Please stop and sit still
No more fidgeting, just chill
It's all got too much
I've had enough
But you are continually
Talking and snoring in your sleep
Mouth forever open chewing as you eat
Dropping clothes on the carpet
Dirty, smelly socks in the corner
Leaving the loo lid open,
Not flushing a certain number
Peeing on the tiled floor
Clipping yellow toenails through the open door
Drinking straight from a carton
Joking and teasing and not saying pardon
Not changing the loo roll leaving a last sheet
Toothpaste on the mirror
Not soaking pans in the sink
Not listening when I speak
Having to tell you again farther in the week
Becoming very lazy
Hygiene becoming very hazy
And man you really are beginning to stink

But you remind me that this is a two way street
Could it be me that's not very neat?

Spray tan marking the sofa
Hair dye spotting the toilet seat
Turning up the heat a few more degrees
Sitting in our undies baring our knees
Long hair blocking the shower
Wet towels on the bed sheet
Hoovering beneath your feet
Taking selfies with everyone we meet
Time on social media
Never face to face
Always out of place
Toast crumbs in the butter
Butter in the jam
I really should learn to plan

However we can both be very rude
We both ignore each other whilst on the phone
We both have a tendency to just stare
We both like to hog the comfy chair
Or keep hold of the TV remote control
Neither one of us are particularly very cool
We can be as bad as one another
We both say dammit, and bugger
Maybe we truly belong to each other?

FOR THOSE REACHING
THE END

THE MONSTER UNDER THE STAIR

She silently glides into view
The talons slide round the door
The claws catch in the fibres
Of the carpet laid out on the floor
We can hear its breath rasping
The click of its teeth
Snatching, scratching, gnashing
Not fast, slowly at best
Surely it's not true
Please don't jest
We try not to look
Its easier we don't stare
But our ears can still hear
And the noxious fumes that rise from the netherworld
Once were buried now unfurled
Its death that lingers in the air
Waking up in its lair
Though everybody has seen her
Everybody knows she is here
We still assume she's not there
We pretend we don't care
But there's a spider living under the stair
And sometimes out of nowhere
She jumps and shrieks and lands in your hair

AAAAAAHHHHHH!!!!

FEAR

My gran had Alzheimer's
My dad had dementia
I felt I was getting the same
The feelings that flow through me
Afraid I'm going insane

In me I could sense the fear
The results I was afraid to hear
But the doctor sat me in front
And looked up from his notes

And declared
Its not as bad as we feared
But there's something I have to declare
With you I have to share

It happens to us all
I suffer from the same
But nobody can take the blame
I'm sorry to say

I'll try and tell you with care
There's nothing I or you can do
That I'm afraid simply put
I'm afraid it's just your age

My dear!

I'M TRYING TO WRITE.....

I'm trying to write a poem like Pam Ayres
As she walks round the house
As she trudges up the stairs

Hers are a mite daft and a little confusing
But her compositions are very amusing
She's very good at finding the right words
At just the right times
Like musical scales with musical chimes

She can write about herself
And how she's getting older
She's a self-deprecator
A self-appreciator
She laughs at the truth
With her senseless kind of mirth

With her voice that evokes a memory
Of 'that's life' once on the telly
Enunciating scintillating words that we applaud
When so perfectly pronounced
Or is it that we clapped ourselves
When we all understand the verse

She has a way about her
That's so hard to beat
She draws on whatever crosses her mind
Her imagination comes alive
And gives us such an artistic treat

She has a way with the sounds
That I can't figure out
They stream from her pen
They trip from her mouth

She's a clever old stick
As her thoughts come at a lick
Every line is quite sublime
I really don't see how they come to mind

Where does she find the time
To write such comedic lines
I wish I had the prose
I pray to gain the airs
But I haven't got what she's got

I haven't got the flairs
I haven't got the characters to make them all rhyme
I haven't got the stories and tales
Although I'm sure they'll come in time

I haven't got a family that I can rant about
I haven't got any pets
A cat a dog or a fish
That are really rude that I can joke about

I admire Pam Ayres
She is my favourite poet
But I'll never tell her
She may not ever know it

But if you see her on stage
In her one woman show
Clap your appreciation
As she takes a curtsy or an appreciative bow

And for a little while longer you'll nod
Because you now know the world will be fine
So go out have a laugh
And just enjoy the rest of your time

I've tried to write a poem like Pam Ayres
But it'll take me a little while
As I haven't got her style
However I really don't mind
Because I know I'm sure
I think that very soon
I will definitely, yes certainly
categorically, indubitably find mine

I'll carry on trying to write a poem like Pam Ayres
As I walk through the house
As I trudge up the stairs

CHRISTMAS CHOICES

It must be nearly a year
Twelve months at least I fear
Where the winter season is so very near
A time to spend with all the family
A time to look forward
We hope it's not a calamity
Where grievances are lost and found
Where petty arguments stir abound and around
A time to celebrate with those we've lost touch
Though for some, not very much
Which one of our homes will we be staying?
Which one of our parents will be doing the baking?
Do we have to choose?
Because one of them must surely lose
However, what if we are daring?
Just this once lets not do the sharing
Let's get away, as we've considered before
Because we all know our cousins will be a terrible bore
Let the relatives do their own thing
Whilst we spend time on a couples fling
Go aboard a ship for a cruise
Or climb the steps to a plane with nothing to lose
Leaving imprints on a soft sandy beach
Wearing tee shirts and shorts and baring our knees
Whilst the warm Caribbean current blows
Water lapping around our toes
Our bodies burning red all over
That's the way it usually goes
Or should we experience the really chilly weather?
As we wrap up warm on a skiing adventure
Wooden chalets as our home

Videoing the snow boarding falls on our phone
We fill our heads with dreams as before
We fill our hearts with a little more
Of course it will never happen
The reality we realise is a chore
We will organise the festivities
Hang all the decorations
Bring in the tree
Root it to the floor

Prepare all the lists
Wrapping all the gifts
Laying out the table
Cooking the vast fayre
Decide who sits on which chair
This year as with the last we will be the hosts
We've written all the invitations
We've sent them through the post
We will have the biggest party
There will be no rival
It will be the best of the most
Especially when we finish with our potent sherry trifle
Then when it's all over
We can congratulate each other
It really has been the feast of times
We've listened to the Queen
As the bells of Big Ben chimes
Most of the relatives have gone
All we have left are the raw turkey groans
There's grandpa slipping off the chair
And grandma sleeping off the beer
The children are playing with the wrapping
And aunt and uncle were caught upstairs napping?

BONG!!

We'd wish we'd done it different
But now that we are here
We wouldn't change a thing
If only we could, my dear
We lift our glasses and then we cheer

MERRY CHRISTMAS AND A HAPPY NEW YEAR

This time we didn't get away
Instead we had the family to stay
Of the choices we had
It was made very clear
I'm sure we'll look forward to it all again, next year

Oh no; Oh dear

A PREGNANT PAUSE

Here's to the midwife who delivered our child
All through the best of times
All through the worst of times
All through those times that felt so wild

Here's to the lady who delivered our baby
All with no fuss, all with no qualm
She held her so gently
Then placed her so softly within our loving arms

THE NATIONAL HEALTH SYSTEM

Here's to the NHS a fine British institution
We are automatic members
We should be glad of its inclusion
Here's to the staff
The real people, who make it what it is
The nurses, doctors and receptionists
The ones we see, our first defence
But lets not forget the other workers
The cleaners, the cooks, the day and night porters
Those that work so hard behind the scenes
Without them no one else up front
Will of course never be seen
We are glad we have it when we need it
However we should try not to abuse it
We could try not to misuse it
For minor scrapes, colds and flu
Try approaching a chemist
A pharmacist before you do
Always be polite and courteous when you visit
Everyone there is there for you
You may have to wait
So be a little patient
They are doing what they can
To help you through the queue
So please no more complaining
Getting on your high horse
Stand up and give a big cheer
Without them some of us wouldn't be living
Some of us wouldn't even be here

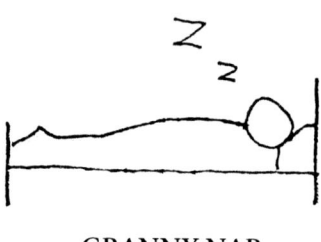

GRANNY NAP

My daughter is lovely
I really can't complain
But when she goes off to work
She leaves her children behind

I don't always mind
But sometimes I find
I'm used as a skivvy, an unpaid nanny
Sometimes I wish I wasn't so kind

It seems nice I guess
But at times I'm feeling a little bereft
Because as your mum It's not very befitting
To always be expected to help with the babysitting

The four year old is talking
The two year old is in a scream
I know she's not doing it on purpose
I know she's not that mean
The little one is a continuous number two machine

I'm forever explaining, changing
Fast forward entertaining
Washing, cooking, feeding
I've just had enough it's my day off you're stealing

When I try to object
I become so guilty I feel so crap
My minds in a mess I'm getting in a flap
For all of this I sacrificed my regular afternoon

Granny nap

I really adore my house
That I share with my loving spouse
But since he's finished work
I realise I'm living with a jerk

I wish he hadn't retired
As he's making my life very tired
He follows me round the home
He never ever leaves me alone

You missed a bit here
You've left a bit there
I'm sure you've done better
Oh! You poor, poor dear

I'm now run off my feet, I need my sleep
I wish he'd go away, talk to another sap
So I can just turn in and lay
For my long deserved for afternoon

Granny nap

My chums, the girls are a god-send
They truly are my best friends
We meet once a week
With them around life's not so bleak

We go to a social club
Occasionally we visit the local pub
It's the break that we need
From our own family

We'll pass round the cakes, the treats
We'll sip our strong brewed coffees and teas
We'll try to talk about religion and politics
But we'd rather have a chat and do some gossiping

As we talk through the minutes
As we converse through the hours
We start to yawn and lose our powers
Falling into a slumber
With our coats on our laps
As we all have to admit
We all enjoy those collective afternoon

Granny naps

FOR THOSE WHO
SHOULD KNOW BETTER

(PLEASE LETS ALL START TO WORK TOGETHER)

WHAT A COLOSSAL MESS

I'm sure we can afford
To give more for those who are poor
But people; don't expect it on sight
We have to work for the right
Don't expect it to be handed out on a plate
As you are not the governments mate
Apply for what you are entitled for
But don't cheat when you haven't the right to more

However government don't mess with legislation
Don't put off the laws to help our nation
Don't give out promises
Then fade them away
Achieve what you pledged
And what you repeated every single day
Finish what you set out to do
As we all believed and voted for you

We are all getting bored
When you spend the money we haven't on board
On something we don't want
On something we don't need
On something we can't afford
Leave those pet projects behind
Spend it on something more useful
On something that we really mind

Don't waste money flushing it down the loo
Find a cheaper version that's what you should do
Don't pander to rich companies
Don't accept the bonuses awarded to you
Or the pay-rises you give yourself
That are far, far, far more than the rest of us

At the moment in this world of austerity
We feel you are not, well, not very worthy

All the businesses that are going bust
All the jobs that are lost
All the workers are taking a loss
Where the owners and managers don't give a toss
The millions they award themselves
When their companies are going down
Leaving us all with a permanent frown

The directors have plenty
Because their workers are on empty
Leaving us with no chances
Not able to balance our finances
Taking away the pensions we've earned
These are lessons that should have been learned
Just do what's right for all of us
Then maybe we won't kick up a fuss

Stop arguing amongst yourselves
Don't spend time blaming each other
Instead start working closer together
Begin by taking advice from new experts
Instead of listening to the usual
Yes and no man jerks
Try doing something more practical
Show us something more factual
Come on politicians sitting on the back benches
You should be ashamed
Perching precariously on the narrow fences

However we don't want you to be bullied
We don't want you to feel you are under duress
As you go off on your long annual holidays

Leaving the rest of us to deal with the stress
Just don't accept from those who are wrong
Let's compose a new tune
Sing a different song
Try to stand up for yourself
And let's sort out this colossal mess

WERE YOU BULLIED?

Those bullies at school they weren't so clever
Those bullies in your youth
They weren't no never
They felt they had the upper hand
Strutting their self in front of their moronic band
They jeered and laughed and acted the clown
They harassed and spat and beat you down
It went on so long
And you knew it was wrong
However you tried to wait them out
To bide your time
Maybe their homelife wasn't so fine
Now these bullies are using twitter
But their spelling and diction has got no better
Where are these bullies now
That still aren't clever
They are now trolling in their bedrooms
Where they have no life
No not ever
But you pulled up your socks
You've left school behind you
You are now an extremely confident you
And although it caused you strife
You haven't let it ruin your life
You now understand
That for all of us it was tough
You are now the one that's successful
You are now the one that can have the last laugh

THE DEVIL INSIDE

There's a dark sludge
Running underneath your white façade
And you should hang your head in shame
I hope you make retribution for your acts
I hope you take the blame
If you don't feel guilt for the rest of your life
Than you are not who I thought you were
You seemed so innocent
An angel blessed
Now the evidence is against you
Your halo has slipped
You've gone too far
You thought you had created a good and honest shell
You tried to suggest you were from the light of heaven
Instead you reside in the black pits of hell
All these years you've acted the martyr
Now you've become reckless
You've been quite feckless
No more is there armour
We've all seen inside
You cannot hide
The saint has left the dance floor
And now forever silently walks out the door

FOR THOSE WHO
WISH A LITTLE MORE

PLEASE MIND THE GAP

Please mind the gap

The next train to arrive on platform 3
Will be the 10.32 currently on time
Oh no I'm sorry to the passengers waiting for the 10.32
I'm afraid there will now be a short delay
As the wrong kind of leaves are on the line
This train is now expected to depart at 10.59
Whilst at this station if you notice anything auspicious
A bag or a case left on its own
Or a person who looks suspicious
Please call the British Transport Police
Or inform any member of staff that you see
Do not approach as it may be a bomb
Thanks for letting us know, I'm sure we won't be long
I remind travellers this is a non-smoking platform
Please extinguish all cigarettes
As it's not very healthy
And it causes such a mess
Please try to conform
Show a little class
Please no running at this station
I guess that also includes no walking on the grass
Don't be in such a hurry
We want you to be careful
We don't want you tripping and falling on your ass
When stepping on the train
Take all your belongings with you
Don't leave any behind
No longer do we have a lost property office
To store your forgotten luggage
We now destroy all known baggage

The train now approaching platform 3
Is the delayed 10.32
Now expected to depart at 11.03
The train consists of four carriages
First class at the front
For those who can afford the outrageous prices
And place wheelchairs, prams, pushchairs and bicycles
Near the toilet cubicles located at the back
We wish you a safe journey
And once more we remind you

PLEASE MIND THE GAP

HAM, EGG AND CHIPS

Ham, egg and chips
That's what I'll be having
It's better than sausage and mash
And steak and kidney pudding

Life wouldn't be worth living
Without ham, egg and chips
It truly is my favourite dish
I add it every year to my Xmas wish list

Korma or vindaloo
Or a Chinese dinner wouldn't do
A ready-made frozen meal
Is not my preferred ideal

Neither is fish caught on a reel
Crumbed or battered in vegetable oil
Of course I'm always being told to help save the planet
By becoming a veggie or vegan

But dammit
I understand I should give it a go
My own organic food I should grow
But although I shouldn't, I'll just say NO!

Grasshoppers and crickets
The world sees the future protein on a plate
But it doesn't sound like a fantastic date
Legs and wings stuck in your teeth
They're not coming anywhere near my fat cheeks

But I'll tell you
If I'm going out for a snack
I'll never turn my back
It's always ham, egg and chips

My belly I'll feed
Although I might
Sometimes very occasionally
Add some mighty nutritious Heinz baked beans

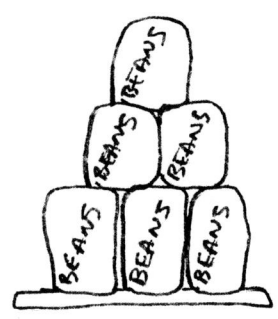

THE SHOPPING TROLLEY

See the trollies
A weekly shop
What they contain
Shouldn't come as a shock
Pizzas, burgers, chips
Ready for frying
A small bag of spinach
I see they're trying
Fizzy drinks and handy snacks
A chock load of sugar
A large amount of fats
Over the years our diets have changed
Over time our bodies are strained
Internal organs can't cope
Lives held on a thread of a rope
Exercise belongs in the past
The couch now our heroes are cast
We workout the remote control
The mobile phone
The games consul
Voices obsolete
Text the new way to speak
Fingers type softly over the keys
Millions of friends
None that we see
The thought of going out
Fill us with fear
Work and sustenance a click
Then it's here

Life expectancy once on the rise
Starting to fall
No real surprise
Diabetes, heart attacks, strokes
And after we croak
Think of the parents who lay you to rest
Never before heard the line
We must confess
It's now to them
We should remember to bless

MYSELF, I AND ME

Who am I?
It's become a heavy task
But it's a question we sometimes need to ask
It's not for me you understand
It's for the forms we fill in
For the surveys to be a part in
We need an identity
I know it makes sense
These days the choice is truly immense
I don't see me as a man or a woman
A him or a her
A boy or a girl
A husband or a wife
A mother or a father
Or rather?
I could be any kind of gender
We've all read the hype
Over one hundred types
I can now choose who I wish to be
And whoever we are
We should all be treated with dignity
In this multi-sexual world
There is a list that's come my way
I've gone through them one at a time
But I don't agree
I've decided who I am
And that's just I, myself
Yes, I'm the one and only me

THE TEA WRITER

I write all my poems in coffee shops
It's where most of the poets started their hopes
I lay the paper on the table
This is where I'll begin an extraordinary fable
I write one word then two, then three, then four
I'll finish a verse and then even more
I look around at all the people
Drinking their mochas, cappuccinos and cafe au lait
But I've always been a simple man
For me it's always been
A pot of freshly brewed Indian tea
I often wonder when they look at me
What they are thinking
When I bend forward to jot down what I see
Then I'm surprised when a staff member
Asks if I'd like another cup of tea
It seems I'm going to get it free
They act very polite
They speak very proper
They think I'm writing a report
As a secret shopper
When I've finished my tea has turned cold
But I slurp it cool as I can't stand the waste

On something that I've been sold
After all it's cost me money
To be exact two pound ten
I've done it a few times before
I'm sure I'll do it a few times again
However, when I get up to leave
I've found I've got to stop
I can't depart the shop
You see now; I've drunk TOO much tea
So I now have to visit the loo
As I'm now dying for a poo
And a pee

ATMOSPHERE

A splash as red as a Mediterranean hue
Large monochrome pictures old but new
Atmospheres hard to beat
Clattering of plates
Pots pouring teas
Feast of sweetie snacks, savoury too
Pastries, cakes, muffins of blue
Free paper from a rack
Chocolate dusted decaf
Loud laughs, soft murmurs
Background voices
Coffee smells
Soft lighting
Brick faced walls
Dark dusty corners
Peoples of ones or twos
Families exchanging news
Dogs by feet
Leather covered seats
Real oak floors
Inward opening doors
Passing traffic
High screeched racket
Trays of dirty dishes
Tasty breakfast wishes
Push chairs
Wheelchairs
High chairs
Soft chairs, just a few
Baristas fussing over you
Toilets in the corners

What's the codes?
Time to unload
Checking face book, twitter, a note or two
Romantic trysts conversing together
What's your pleasure?
Milk on tray?
Semi-skimmed, full fat
Soya, oat or almond to try
Would you like anything with that?
Maybe our new vegan range?
To meat lovers it makes a change
Come every morning, noon and early nights
We welcome your visit for a coffee lovers delight

CORONA VIRUS BLUES

Remember when we were social
And not so distant
Remember when we used to give a hug
Hold a hand, kiss a cheek
Remember the time we met our friends
In shops, cafes, round our homes, in garden pubs
When we talked about something and nothing
Going out every day
Travelling on a bus or a train and going away
Remember when we weren't on furlough
Workmates by our side
Where we would greet
Say hello, how are you and hi
Remember the shopping
Whether buying or window hopping
Meeting up together not in ones or twos
But threes, fours, fives or sixes
And with anyone else we choose
Remember when grandparents came round for tea
For talking about school, playing and watching TV
Remember when we gathered together in the park
Catching some rays
"now sir, please move on, not anymore, not today"
When lovers were face to face
In each other's arms, in the same place
Singing and dancing on the same floor
Remember when we had a little more
But now we're kind to our neighbours
Cheering our saviours
Our classrooms, our restaurants, our gyms
Are now in our homes
With thousands of rainbows decorating our roads

Entertaining each other walking for charity
We've now all seen the clarity
Maybe out of this there's something we can learn
Giving us a chance to teach
We're all beginning to be patient
Two metres away on the street
We're starting to become more polite
Waiting in a queue "please after you"
Could that really be the point?
When this is over
Will the world change for the better?
Will we begin to trust?
Reaching for hope, surely it must
Will our countries start living together?
Will our enemies become friends?
Needing each other
It must be about time
It's well overdue
We can't wait for it to be over
This epidemic affecting me and you
Maybe in the future we'll look back and say
Do you remember that year of 2020?
The age of the Corona Virus Blues

AT LAST IT'S FINISHED

INDEX OF FIRST LINES